THE WIDENING CIRCLE

THE WIDENING CIRCLE

EXTENSION AND CONTINUING EDUCATION AT THE UNIVERSITY OF ALABAMA, 1904–1992

Jeanie Thompson

THE UNIVERSITY OF ALABAMA

COLLEGE OF CONTINUING STUDIES

TUSCALOOSA, ALABAMA

The paper on which this book is printed meets the minimum requirements of
American National Standard for Information Science—Permanence of Paper for
Printed Library Materials, ANSI Z39.48—1984.

Library of Congress Catalog card number: 92-61798

Thompson, Jeanie (Jean F.)
The widening circle: extension and continuing education at The University of
Alabama, 1904-1992 / Jeanie Thompson.
p. cm.
ISBN 0-9634589-06

First Edition

*This book is dedicated
to the memory of*

BYRD THOMAS THOMPSON, JR.,

a lifelong learner.

CONTENTS

PREFACE

The University of Alabama's College of Continuing Studies began as the Extension Division in 1919. It has been in continuous operation since that time, evolving from the Extension Division to Extended Services in 1970 to Division of Continuing Education in 1977. In 1983 it became a full-fledged academic unit and was renamed the College of Continuing Studies.

The College's programs serve clienteles as diverse as government employees, professional groups, and business and industry professionals, as well as traditional and non-traditional students, faculty, and professional administrators. Through credit and noncredit programs offered in a variety of formats, the College of Continuing Studies extends the resources of The University of Alabama to those who wish to continue learning.

Nationally, and even internationally, as the concept of *extension* has evolved into the broader concept of *continuing education*, an ever-widening circle of people has been offered access to knowledge. In her book, *Expanding Access to Knowledge: Continuing Higher Education*, Rae Wahl Rohfeld writes about this American passion for knowledge and its natural connection with higher continuing education:

Americans have always looked to education as the means for preserving what was valuable in life and for transforming what needed to be improved. From protecting religion in New England towns to enhancing civic virtue in colonial and early national cities; from individual fulfillment to societal redirection—education has seemed the means by which all was possible. University extension has played a central role in the process of expanding people's access to education. In large part, the history of university extension—of higher continuing education—is the story of increasing access to knowledge to ever more diverse audiences (1).

The extension and continuing education movement at The University of Alabama parallels the movement's development nationally in a number of ways. One primary way centers on the Division of Continuing Education, which later became the College of Continuing Studies, acknowledging that the part-time, adult student population was increasing and would indeed out-distance the traditional 18–22-year-old population by the year 2000, if not before. Recognizing this phenomenon, the division set about to plan programs and offer non-traditional formats for learning that would make gaining further education — or acquiring education for the first time — easier for adults. Since the early 1970s those working in extended services and continuing education have been the champions for this rapidly growing, yet extremely diverse, student population.

This book attempts to chronicle the development of extension, the evolution of extended services, and the blossoming of continuing education on the campus of The University of Alabama. While many specific programs, names, places, and events have been documented, many others have not been included simply because of time and space considerations. Still, it is hoped that the reader will gain insight into the development of what started as a service and has now evolved over some 88 years into a vital aspect of The University of Alabama.

As technological advances push us toward constantly updating our education, it is the continuing education specialists on any college campus who perhaps stand most ready to meet the challenges of a highly technologically advanced world. Thus the widening circle becomes a true sphere as our possibilities for continuing education evolve toward global impact. This book celebrates all who work, or have worked, in continuing education for The University of Alabama. Their contributions are herein recognized.

Acknowledgements

I n 1973, Dr. Galen Drewry, then associate academic vice-president for Extended Services, commissioned a history of extension service at The University of Alabama. Jill Fussell apparently reviewed documents in the archives, including a history begun in the 1940s by Clarice Parker, and interviewed a number of individuals to produce a draft history covering approximately 1902–73. Internal memos from 1973 indicate that the Fussell draft was reviewed and that the chapter covering 1969–73 was deleted. The history was evidently not published in final form.

In 1990, Dr. John C. Snider, dean of the College of Continuing Studies, approached me about writing a history of the College. Robert Horner, a graduate student in English and participant in the College's EASE program, assisted with preliminary research and editing for the project. Robert uncovered the Fussell draft carefully preserved in a drawer in Bettie Copeland's desk (Bettie was assistant budget director at the time). He corroborated this draft against existing archives, and after editing and updating, we feel confident that it represents a reasonably accurate picture of the emergence and growth of extension at The University of Alabama from 1904–69. This constitutes Part I of the book.

Part II covers Dr. Drewry's era until the present day, 1969–

92, and has been drafted using annual reports to the President, interviews, brochures, documents in the College's archives, and other sources of University history. A bibliography of materials consulted is included.

This book could not have been completed without the invaluable assistance of Bettie Copeland. Her tenacious digging through files to find dates, names, and summary reports was enormously helpful.

A number of individuals helped with research or fact-checking, or read drafts of the manuscript. Within the college I would like to thank Reggie Smith, Duane Cunningham, and Robert Hudson for reading sections of the draft for factual accuracy. Every director, and many other staff members, in the College contributed information and answered questions. From the College of Communication I would like to thank Keith Barze for giving of his time to research ETV and other history relating to communication and Jim Oakley for checking my facts relating to the Alabama Press Association and the News Bureau.

I would like to thank a number of others within the College who provided technical expertise: Loranette Collier obtained documents from archives, and, Loranette, Reggie Smith, Wendy Tidmore, Kelsey Reon, and Katie Carlton all braved the sixth floor of Martha Parham West in search of documents for the history. Wendy also ably prepared typescript. Clara Smith patiently assisted with the print production process of the book; Reata Strickland offered advice in the areas of graphics research and production; Jill West and Todd Lambert assisted with extensive photo research; Wendy Wilkerson researched and assisted with writing the current day chapter. Bill Golightly provided expert editorial support for the entire manuscript. Bouquets to everyone else in the College of Continuing Studies who lent moral support and were patient while this project came to life.

I am also grateful to Lisa Rhiney of University Relations for researching photographs and to Rickey Yanaura for reproducing archival photographs. Joyce Lamont, Clark Center, and Gunetta Rich, in the William Stanley Hoole Special Collections Library of the Amelia Gayle Gorgas Library located extension archives and photographs.

Special thanks to Paula Dennis for her expertise in book design and production, and her grace under pressure. Anne Gibbons proofed and indexed the text and I am very grateful for her talent in this regard.

I also greatly appreciate the editorial assistance of Katherine Thompson who read and offered comments on the manuscript.

And finally, to all those former employees I interviewed in the process, a heartfelt thank-you for sharing your history and yourselves so that I might make the picture clearer.

JT

FOREWORD

I n 1907 when President John Abercrombie defined his vision for the future of The University of Alabama in his blueprint, "The Greater University," he set the stage for 88 years of progressive, innovative, and expanding university extension or continuing education.

Continuing education has proved to be a rather positive—albeit complex—programming concept over the years and has played an extremely important outreach role at The University of Alabama throughout its history. Whether officially titled continuing studies, extension, extended studies, or just service, the function of carrying knowledge to the residents of Alabama and surrounding areas has always prevailed in one form or another at the institution.

The field of continuing higher education as a professional practice is essentially not well understood by the public in general. Most Americans whose exposure to continuing education has been limited to one or two programming experiences find the field to be a rather perplexing mosaic. Hence, the purpose of this history might be stated as twofold: the delineation of the historical evolvement of continuing education at The University of Alabama, and the further clarification of the multidimensional nature of the practice. Indeed, it is the intent of this book to advance our understanding of both the growth and development of professional continuing education at Alabama, that is, the widening circle.

John C. Snider
Dean
College of Continuing Studies
The University of Alabama
October 1992

The Widening Circle

PART 1

THE BEGINNING AND GROWTH OF EXTENSION AT THE UNIVERSITY OF ALABAMA

1904–1969

CHAPTER 1

PREPARING ALABAMA'S EDUCATORS

1904–1919

The precise beginning of the extension effort at The University of Alabama is difficult to pinpoint. In his *History of the University of Alabama, Volume One,* (1953) James B. Sellers recounts turn-of-the-century attempts at extension that include local weekend lectures on literary topics and an unsuccessful effort on the part of the Board of Trustees to coerce faculty into teaching summer school. Sellers notes that the 1898–99 catalog mentions serious extension work in literature and that in the following year lectures in elocution, law, and the legal status of the medical profession were offered on campus.

Perhaps the place to begin is with the earliest formal attempts at extension service for educators.

When former Alabama state superintendent of education Dr. John W. Abercrombie became president of The University of Alabama in 1902, he was well aware that Alabama needed more and better schools with properly trained teachers. Few school teachers had college educations. Usually someone who completed high school (which at the time extended no further than the eleventh grade) remained to teach the lower grades, gradually growing into the position his former teacher held. The typical teacher could teach little more than the basics of reading, writing, and arithmetic.

President John W. Abercrombie focused on teacher education and officially began the University's extension efforts.

PRESIDENT JOHN W. ABERCROMBIE, 1902

A brief but careful study undertaken by the University revealed that the institution reflected the poor showing made by education in the state. Its professional schools (law and medicine) admitted students with less academic training than was required for the liberal arts college. Admission standards to the liberal arts college were not stringent. Graduates of a first-class secondary school could enter the sophomore class, but there were few such high schools in the state.

In 1902, the University had 375 students and 43 faculty members. Its physical plant was inadequate even with the small enrollment. Support was so limited that monies coming in from royalties and the sale of coal lands, properly belonging in the permanent funds of the University, were exhausted in meeting the costs of current operations.

1902

JOHN W. ABERCROMBIE, FORMER ALABAMA SUPERINTENDENT OF EDUCATION, BECOMES PRESIDENT OF THE UNIVERSITY OF ALABAMA.

HOOLE SPECIAL COLLECTIONS

IN 1904, THE FIRST SIX-WEEKS-LONG SUMMER SCHOOL WAS HELD AT THE
UNIVERSITY OUTDOORS UNDER CANOPIES.

Yet with all these limitations, President Abercrombie had a
vision of where the University might go. He drew upon the
limited funds available and had blueprints drawn up for the
University of the future, a "Greater University."

First Summer School, 1904

One of Abercrombie's first requests for legislative aid,
readily granted by the state legislature in 1903, was for a
modest appropriation to conduct a summer school for Alabama school teachers on the University campus. The first six-
week-long summer school in 1904 drew 351 students. During
the next few years summer school attendance dropped by 50
or 100 students until 1912, when attendance jumped to 517.
(Part of this increase was probably due to faculty resolutions
that enlarged summer school to include regular University
students and those who needed to upgrade their education
before they were allowed to enter the University as regular
students.)

President Abercrombie's "Greater University" began to

evolve in 1907 with help from the Alabama legislature. It voted an appropriation of $400,000 to be used for erecting new buildings on campus between 1907 and 1910. It was during these years that Smith Hall (used as the geological and natural history museum and for lectures and labs for the Geology and Biology departments), Comer Hall (used as the engineering building), and Morgan Hall (used as the main academic building) were built.

Dr. Abercrombie, A One-Man Extension Division

As state superintendent of education, Dr. Abercrombie had become aware of the national trend toward extension on university and college campuses and of the "Wisconsin idea" of extension, which was a current model around the nation. During his first years at the University, President Abercrombie served as a one-man extension division, traveling to nearly every county and city in the state, delivering addresses before every kind of gathering and meeting with schools and local and state teachers' conventions.

At first many of the University's faculty members were reluctant to help him, believing it was not befitting the dignity of a college professor to do so. A few, however, understood the President's vision and began helping Dr. Abercrombie promote better educational opportunities for Alabama's youth.

About the time that the summer school was established, a University field representative began promoting development and standardization of Alabama's high schools and colleges. In many respects, this was the beginning of extension service by The University of Alabama—helping state and local authorities develop better schools.

1910-11

A SUMMER SCHOOL FOR PUBLIC SCHOOL TEACHERS IS FOUNDED (270 ENROLLED).

Closely associated with President Abercrombie in these pioneer efforts were Dr. Edward F. Buchner, professor of philosophy and education (1903–8); Joel C. DuBose, high school visitor (1905–7); Dr. Fletcher B. Dresslar, professor of philosophy and education (1908–11) and dean of the School of Education (1910–11); and Dr. James J. Doster, who was appointed in 1907 and served as high school visitor, professor of philosophy and education, and then dean of the College of Education (1911–42).

Hoole Special Collections

President George H. Denny, 1911

When Dr. Abercrombie left in 1911, Dr. George H. Denny, formerly president of Washington and Lee University, came to The University of Alabama as president. The same year, Dr. Doster became dean of the College of Education.

1911

George H. Denny becomes President of the University.

President Denny had gained first-hand experience in fund-raising at Washington and Lee. Bringing this valuable knowledge with him, he took a great interest in the University's finances and built up an endowment fund.

Faculty Lectures, 1912

James J. Doster

President Denny and Dean Doster arranged for special groups of lectures beginning in 1912–13. As first announced in the University catalog, these bimonthly lectures were primarily intended for University engineering students but were open to the public. They brought prominent railroad officials, manufacturers, engineers, and specialists to the University to give papers.

In the following year, the catalog indicates that many of the 50 lectures in education, history, literature, science, and

1916-17

Term-time classes in further education for public school teachers.

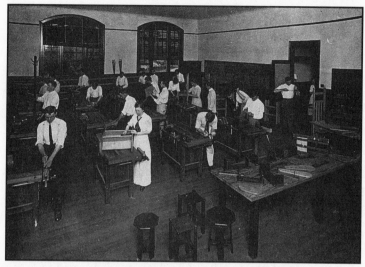

THE SCHOOL OF EDUCATION'S VOCATIONAL EDUCATION DEPARTMENT BEGAN
PROVIDING MANUAL TRAINING FOR SHOP TEACHERS IN WOOD WORKING,
MECHANICAL DRAWING, AND RELATED AREAS BY 1918.

math were given by University professors. President Denny
and Dean Doster lectured on education.

These lectures were one of the building blocks for a formal
extension division. They were no doubt used to sell the need
of better education to Alabamians, in addition to simply
extending a higher level of knowledge to the public.

First Extension Classes, 1917

In 1917, Dean Doster organized the first extension classes
in Birmingham. In 1918, the School of Education's Vocational
Education Department began providing training for shop
teachers through extension classes. For those already on the
job teaching shop to Alabama's young men, professional
training was arranged in trade centers. The University held

1917

FIRST EXTENSION CLASSES IN BIRMINGHAM ORGANIZED BY DR. JAMES J. DOSTER,
FIRST DEAN OF UA'S COLLEGE OF EDUCATION.

courses during summer school for shop teachers. For those who could not attend the University or any of the training centers, the School of Education provided correspondence courses. The school year 1916–17 was the first time extension students were listed in the catalog (it was the custom to list the students at that time)—60 students, all under the School of Education.

An Educational Study of Alabama, 1919

By 1919, the University had plans for the establishment of an Extension Division. But before these plans were formally implemented, *An Educational Study of Alabama* was published by the United States Department of the Interior, Bureau of Education, and presented to the Alabama Education Commission in June 1919.

Reinforcing the need for an extension service, it lamented that the planned budget for the proposed Extension Division at the University was so small:

> There is a great need in the State of Alabama for the general university extension service contemplated by The University of Alabama. The amount of money recommended in its budget is insufficient to do very much. However, it may be all that the University can hope to secure at this time, and it is better to make a beginning so as to demonstrate sufficiently to the people of Alabama the value of extension work possible through their university. In time the extension division at the University should have a large number of practical courses in engineering and commercial subjects, as important to the industrial life of the State of Alabama as agricultural extension is to the agricultural interests of the State. It is equally important that the extension work of The University of Alabama contribute information and training in the cultural subjects and social sciences. (*An Educational Study of Alabama*, published by the U.S. Department of the Interior, Bureau of Education, June 1919).

Beginning of the Extension Division, 1919

The study provided the final impetus to begin an Extension Division at the University. The Alabama Legislature appropriated $5,000 for the fiscal year beginning October 1, 1919, and $7,500 for each year thereafter for a number of years for an Extension Division of The University of Alabama.

The idea of university extension service was not new to Alabamians, especially to people in rural areas. For a decade Alabama Polytechnic Institute (later Auburn University) had operated a farm extension service to promote a more diversified system of farming. In just ten years, county agricultural agents had encouraged noticeable changes in farm production. But the agricultural extension did not have to rely entirely on state funds since the federal government funded a large share of the expenses.

University Income, 1917–1923

Alabama had been a poor state, with other states far ahead in educational funding. The 1917–18 University trustees' *Report to the State Legislature* appealed to the incoming governor and legislature for aid. The report, signed by President Denny, listed the University's only two sources of income: state appropriations, which comprised $25,000 per annum to the University proper, $5,000 per annum to the School of Medicine, and $5,000 per annum to the summer school; and interest from leased lands, amounting to $35,000 per annum. This report was made just a year before the Legislature appropriated $5,000 to begin an Extension Division at the University.

These figures were well below what other states were giving their universities at that time. Wisconsin, Illinois, and Minnesota were funding over $2 million each per annum, and even at the bottom of the scale, Arkansas, North Carolina, Oklahoma, and Virginia were providing between $200,000 and $300,000 each per annum.

> *"There can be no sound reason why The University of Alabama should not be given an opportunity to do such work in its particular field of service. Other states have taken definite action in this direction."*
> —President George H. Denny

President Denny articulated the need for an extension service at the University: "We desire just now merely to call attention to the fact that The University of Alabama lacks the means to perform so obvious a duty as to engage effectively in any single phase of extension work, which constitutes so large and so important a part in a modern university program. This great field of service, by means of which an institution projects its educational forces beyond the campus, is carried on in state universities through various agencies. It is, of course, a fact that the federal and state governments are jointly supplying funds whereby the agricultural colleges are enabled to do valuable extension work in their particular sphere of activity. There can be no sound reason why The University of Alabama should not be given an opportunity to do such work in its particular field of service. Other states have taken definite action in this direction."

This strong plea from President Denny in the 1917–18 trustees' report to the legislature was effective. The 1919 legislature appropriated to the University $121,000 for 1919–20, increasing to $165,000 for 1922–23. This included funds for the Extension Division, the summer school, and the School of Medicine. In addition, $115,000 was appropriated for buildings on campus.

1919

THE STATE LEGISLATURE APPROVES $5000 IN APPROPRIATIONS FOR AN EXTENSION PROGRAM, NOTING THAT "IN TIME THE EXTENSION DIVISION AT THE UNIVERSITY SHOULD HAVE A LARGE NUMBER OF PRACTICAL COURSES IN ENGINEERING AND COMMERCIAL SUBJECTS AS IMPORTANT TO THE INDUSTRIAL LIFE OF THE STATE OF ALABAMA AS AGRICULTURAL EXTENSION IS TO THE AGRICULTURAL INTERESTS OF THE STATE."

CHAPTER 2

A COMMITMENT TO
ADULT LEARNERS

Era of Dr. James S. Thomas, 1919–1930

T he Extension Division began on a modest budget of $5,000 the first year and operated on $7,500 for a number of succeeding years. Knowing that state funding would be hard to increase, President Denny was determined to make the Extension Division as self-supporting as possible.

Dr. James S. Thomas, a professor of secondary education at the University since 1912 and a high school visitor for many years, was appointed director of the newly formed Extension Division in 1920. Apparently Dr. Thomas was an excellent speaker with a good deal of charisma. He became an effective public relations man for the Extension Division.

Announcement of Extension Division in Catalog

The 1919–20 University catalog announced that The University of Alabama would begin an Extension Division in the 1920–21 school year. It would represent the College of Arts and Sciences, the College of Engineering, the School of Commerce and Business Administration, and the School of Education. The introductory statement said that the University was supported by all of the people of Alabama and that the Extension Division had been established to give the high-

CCS

DR. JAMES S. THOMAS

est educational service possible to the people of the entire
state.

Initially Dr. Thomas and President Denny organized the
Extension Division into two major areas: extension teaching
service and public welfare. Some of the services offered had
been operating already but were placed under the Extension
Division.

Four categories were created under extension teaching service: (1) correspondence study, both credit courses (which a
few teachers had already been offering) and non-credit
directed-reading courses; (2) extension centers for regular
class work, expanding what the School of Education had
started a few years earlier; (3) extension lectures (later called
the Speakers Bureau), which President Denny had encouraged
since 1912, for single lectures or a series of lectures by faculty
members and other available speakers (also available for

1920–21

EXTENSION CLASSES AND CORRESPONDENCE STUDY COURSES ANNOUNCED FOR THE
FIRST TIME IN THE UNIVERSITY CATALOG (DR. JAMES S. THOMAS, FIRST DIRECTOR OF
EXTENSION).

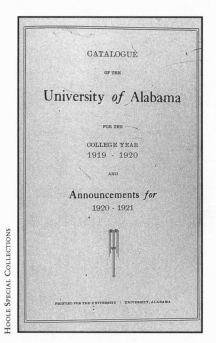

CATALOGUE

OF THE

University *of* Alabama

FOR THE

COLLEGE YEAR
1919 - 1920

AND

Announcements *for*
1920 - 1921

PRINTED FOR THE UNIVERSITY | UNIVERSITY, ALABAMA

commencement addresses and dedications); and (4) club study, with reading and references outlined and directed by a faculty member.

Three categories were listed under public welfare: (1) visual instruction, consisting of films and slides; (2) package libraries, collected materials on almost any subject; and (3) Social Service Institutes (available by request to Alabama's larger population centers) dealing with recreation, juvenile delinquency, child welfare, poverty relief, education, and salesmanship.

Certifying Teachers Through Extension Classes

To keep temporary teaching certificates validated, Alabama elementary and high school teachers had to have as much as six weeks each year of professional study in a standard educational institution, such as the six-week summer session at the University. However, teachers earned very little in those days—white male teachers averaged $440 per year and white female teachers averaged $70 less than that. Black teachers were paid even less. Teachers were able to save very little, and often had to borrow to make it through the summer months. It was difficult for most of them to attend summer school. Of the 12,000 teachers in Alabama in 1920, only 672 attended summer school at the University.

But through the Extension Division, new avenues opened up to help raise the teachers' educational level. Although the

IMPROVING INSTRUCTION TO ALABAMA'S ELEMENTARY AND SECONDARY SCHOOL
TEACHERS THROUGH SUMMER SCHOOL CLASSES WAS A PRIMARY GOAL OF THE EARLY
EXTENSION DIVISION.

Extension Division was also directed to groups other than
teachers, one of its prime objectives was to provide more
educational opportunities for teachers while on the job.

Extension classes, which Dean Doster had started in the
School of Education in 1917, took University professors to
outlying communities to conduct classes, inspiring local
teachers to upgrade themselves. As a framework developed
for teachers to improve themselves, the State of Alabama
could start basing teachers' salaries on the degree of preparation each had. This was one of the recommendations in the
1919 *Educational Study of Alabama.*

During the 1920–21 school year, the first year of formal
operation for the Extension Division, 149 people took advantage of extension classes. No doubt many of these were teachers. As the State Board of Education gradually increased
requirements for teachers, enrollment increased not only in
summer school (jumping to 2,069 the summer of 1922, dropping back to 1,321 in 1925, and climbing again by the summer
of 1929 to 1,871), but also in extension classes (a peak of 2,196

during the 1927–28 school year, dropping to 1,931 by 1928–29).

Many classes were taught by faculty members from the campus and also by instructors stationed in the field, one at Decatur and another at Brewton, who were employed full-time in extension teaching.

CCS

W. C. Crosby founded the Correspondence Study Program, forerunner of the contemporary Division of Independent Study.

Correspondence Study: W. C. Crosby (1923)

Another way for teachers and University students to pick up additional University credit was through correspondence courses. Correspondence study began with limited offerings, probably devised at the request of students.

In 1923, President Denny had appointed W. C. Crosby chief of the Bureau of Visual Instruction under the Extension Division. Crosby soon began improving the correspondence study courses. He visited several institutions already providing correspondence study. Eventually he decided to pattern the University's correspondence procedures more nearly after that of the University of Wisconsin, a pioneer in this field.

In 1923, Crosby published the first UA correspondence study bulletin, outlining standards and procedures and listing 25 courses. Distribution of this bulletin aroused interest in correspondence study among off-campus students and adults educating themselves or wishing to pursue subjects for their cultural values. A mere 37 students were enrolled in correspondence study in 1920–21. But by 1928–29, enrollment had mushroomed to 1,022. Courses were revised as their campus counterparts changed; there was no attempt to maintain an independent curriculum of correspondence courses. Courses were written and graded by faculty members in each particular field.

Club Study

During the decade 1910 to 1920, local groups of teachers were encouraged to become involved in reading circle work. Not only teachers but other club women were attempting serious study of the problems facing the world. Some of this interest was an outgrowth of the famous Chautauqua meetings, which had begun in 1874.

However, lack of adequate Alabama libraries in the state hampered these groups. Only the larger cities had libraries containing material other than fiction and biography, and many of the small towns and rural sections had no libraries at all. In 1920, the club study service began providing directed

1920-29

THE UNIVERSITY AND ITS EXTENSION DIVISION HAVE A PERIOD OF SPECTACULAR GROWTH, WITH EXTENSION COURSES INCLUDING: LECTURES, CORRESPONDENCE STUDY, LIBRARY SERVICES BY MAIL, AUDIO-VISUAL MATERIALS LIBRARY, THE SOCIAL SERVICES INSTITUTE (COURSES IN CHILD WELFARE, RECREATION, JUVENILE DELIN-QUENCY, PROBLEMS OF POVERTY, EDUCATION, AND SALESMANSHIP).

study for these groups. The original club study programs, with the names of the faculty members who prepared them, were

The English Bible .... George Lang
American Society .... Lee Bidgood
Contemporary American Poetry .... Carl Carmer
History of England .... Edmund G. Howe
American Citizenship .... Edmund G. Howe
International Relations .... Edmund G. Howe
Women in Modern Art .... Ruth Parsons
Business Methods of Home Making .... Margaret L. Dozier

"Reading circle" work could be credited toward recertification for teachers, but by 1924 reading circle work for teachers began to decline as the number of extension courses increased. The reading circles which involved teachers interested in recertification remained active only in the counties remote from colleges, where few extension courses were available.

Visual Aids

Although thought to have great promise, visual aids never developed as hoped. Mr. Crosby had been brought to the University because of his specialty in visual aids, and he did promote films and slides for Alabama teachers, but the effort was not successful. There was a lack of suitable projection machines in the state, and the University was unable to budget for appropriate films. The situation grew more difficult until about 1930 when the visual aids service was discontinued. It was later reinstituted in 1941.

1923

W.C. CROSBY, CHIEF OF THE BUREAU OF VISUAL INSTRUCTION OF EXTENSION DIVISION, PUBLISHES THE FIRST CORRESPONDENCE STUDY BULLETIN, LISTING PROCEDURES AND 25 COURSES.

DR. WYATT C. BLASINGAME
SERVED ALABAMA EDUCATION
THROUGH THE EXTENSION
DIVISION FROM 1928–45.

High School Programs

From his contacts in secondary education around the state,
Dr. Thomas developed two high school extension programs in
the late 1920s: high school debates and high school publications. Dr. Wyatt C. Blasingame joined the Extension Division
in 1928 and developed these programs. He retired in 1945.

In 1928–29, the Extension Division joined with the extension divisions of other state universities to form the National
High School Debaters' League. That first year 46 high schools
in the state joined the League under the direction of the
Extension Division, which provided resources for the debaters.

1928

CONTINUING EDUCATION FOR HIGH SCHOOL STUDENTS IS ESTABLISHED (COURSES IN
JOURNALISM, SPEECH, AND MUSIC).

Bessemer High School won the first state championship during the finals held at the University, receiving four University scholarships for qualified Bessemer High School students. By the next year more than 100 high schools had joined the League. In 1958, the Alabama High School Forensic League was formed as an outgrowth of the University debate program.

In 1929–30, the Extension Division (in conjunction with the Department of Journalism) began working with more than 50 high schools to improve their high school yearbooks and newspapers. The number of schools participating in the Alabama High School Publication Association increased in just a few years to more than 100.

In addition, under Dr. Blasingame's supervision, the Extension Division began a Counseling and Guidance Service for high schools, helping students choose an education or occupation best suited to them.

Radio Broadcasting, 1929

The University had been interested in developing a radio station since the early 1920s, but not until 1929 did plans finally materialize under the Extension Division.

Alabama Polytechnic Institute had been broadcasting on and off since 1922. By December 1928, it was operating a well-established radio station, WAPI. The station had just been moved from Auburn to Birmingham in order to serve a majority of the state's population. At the time of the move, The University of Alabama was petitioning the Federal Radio Commission for a license to operate its own station. This led to a joint venture by The University of Alabama, Alabama Polytechnic Institute, and the Alabama College for Women at Montevallo (later University of Montevallo) in the operation of WAPI.

The state legislature determined that The University of Alabama (39%), Alabama Polytechnic Institute (39%), and

FACULTY MEMBERS DISCUSSED WORLD WAR II PEACE PLANS ON A RADIO FORUM BROADCAST BY WAPI.

the Alabama College for Women (22%) should bear the cost of operating WAPI. Dr. Robert E. Tidwell was State Superintendent of Education at this time. In 1929, the station began operating, with The University of Alabama and Alabama Polytechnic Institute providing much of the programming. The University sent professors to Birmingham on a regular basis to broadcast lectures, and Alabama Polytechnic Institute used much of its time for its farm extension program. But with the onset of the depression, the three schools found it necessary to lease the station to commercial interests.

Growth of the Extension Division: 1920–1930

During the 1920s, The University of Alabama had grown tremendously, with much of that growth due to the Extension Division. In 1920–21, only 1,661 students were enrolled in the regular session, with 186 in the Extension Division. By 1928–29, however, 6,106 students were enrolled in the regular session with nearly half of these extension students. The Extension Division had outgrown its office on the south end of the basement of Carmichael Hall and during the 1929–30 school year moved to a three-room suite of offices on the first floor of the newly completed Graves Hall.

Dr. Thomas left the University in 1930 to pursue a full-time public relations career in Birmingham. At this time, President Denny appointed Dr. Robert E. Tidwell, who had been State Superintendent of Education, to fill the vacancy left by Dr. Thomas as director of the Extension Division.

GRAVES HALL, CIRCA 1929

1929–30

EXTENSION DIVISION MOVES TO SUITE OF THREE NEW OFFICES IN RECENTLY COMPLETED GRAVES HALL.

CHAPTER 3

THE GROWTH OF EXTENSION

Era of Dr. Robert E. Tidwell, 1930–1954

When Dr. Robert E. Tidwell came to the University's Extension Division, he brought with him a dozen years experience with the State Department of Education and many years experience as a public school administrator. He had been director of teacher training with the State Department of Education from 1918–27, Assistant Superintendent of Education from 1920 until 1927, and had been elected State Superintendent of Education in 1927. His term as State Superintendent of Education would have ended in 1930, but he left in 1929 to do graduate study at Columbia University. President Denny contacted him while he was at Columbia University, telling him of the vacancy in the Extension Division.

Dr. Tidwell completed his year's study at Columbia before coming to the University in 1930. He was well aware of the changes in teacher certification during the last decade, many of which could be directly credited to him.

Dr. Tidwell's Association with Dr. Abercrombie

Former UA president Dr. John W. Abercrombie, who had put forward the idea of extension lectures at the University, served as State Superintendent of Education from 1920 until

CCS

DR. ROBERT E. TIDWELL

1927. Dr. Abercrombie remained with the State Department of Education, first as Assistant Superintendent of Education from 1927 until 1935, and then as state supervisor of teacher certification from 1935 until his death in 1940.

The close association between Dr. Tidwell and Dr. Abercrombie through the State Department of Education helped Dr. Tidwell after he accepted the appointment as director of the Extension Division in 1930. He was not only aware of the recent teacher training services provided by the University, but also of the early development of extension services.

In 1939, Dr. Tidwell was appointed dean of Extension—the first dean of the division. This recognition put the Extension Division on equal ground with other schools and colleges within the University. Under Dean Tidwell's dynamic leader-

1930

DR. ROBERT E. TIDWELL BECOMES DIRECTOR OF THE EXTENSION DIVISION, LATER ITS FIRST DEAN.

ship, extension classes, correspondence study, and lecture services were flourishing. Audio-visual aids, dramatic and club study services, radio lectures (forerunner of educational radio and television), and high school services were underway.

For two and one-half decades, until 1954, with the full support of President Denny and succeeding presidents, Dean Tidwell's efforts resulted in a tremendous expansion of the University's services to people of the state in all walks of life. By the end of his tenure the following specialized departments in the Extension Division were highly developed and were effectively serving the needs of thousands of people:

Arts and Sciences Extension Services
Audio-Visual Services
Commerce Extension Services
Conference and Short Courses
Correspondence Study (both college and high school courses)
Education Extension (Counseling and Advisory Services)
Engineering Extension Services
Home Economics Extension Services
Library Extension and Program Services
Radio and Television Broadcasting Services
University News Bureau
Resident University Centers (off-campus), including Birmingham, Gadsden, Huntsville, Mobile, and Montgomery
Other Services, which included headquartering on campus and general supervision of the Alabama Press Association and the Alabama Broadcasters Association

The Depression's Effect on The University

In 1927, at the peak of prosperity, the Alabama Legislature had optimistically appropriated substantial increases to educational institutions throughout Alabama for the next four

THE 1930s

COURSES IN EDUCATIONAL BROADCASTING BEGIN.

fiscal years. But shortly after these appropriations were made, it was evident that an economic decline was beginning.

In his 1928 report to the University Board of Trustees, President Denny urged extreme caution in authorizing expenditures pending further developments. He frankly stated that if the Trustees were to adopt the policy of spending everything in sight (even though the University needed every dollar that was available for its operation), the institution might find itself greatly embarrassed if it built a budget based on 1927 conditions.

Luckily, President Denny had the foresight to suspect that state appropriations might fail to materialize. The first indication came shortly after the legislature approved the appropriations in 1927: only $250,000 of a $750,000 appropriation for new buildings was paid in cash; warrants issued for an additional $250,000 remained unpaid.

In the first five months of the 1930–31 school year (with 1930 being the first full year of the depression), the University received only one-fourth of its maintenance appropriation from the state. The tremendous uncertainty regarding finances led to level funding for the 1931–32 budget, with no increases and with the provision that President Denny could, with the approval of the Executive Committee, make such changes as the exigencies of the situation demanded. And he did, out of necessity: the University received only 16 percent of its appropriations in cash during the 1931–32 school year.

Along with other areas of the University, the staff of the Extension Division was reduced. All salaries were cut 10 percent in September 1931 and six months later another 10 percent. And they remained reduced until the 1936–37 school year. All extension teaching was paid for on the basis of fees collected.

Remarkably, although University salaries were cut, they were paid without fail every month during the depression, a feat no other university in the state was able to achieve.

Even with the onset of the depression, enrollment at the

PRESIDENT RICHARD D. FOSTER

University continued to grow, although at a slower rate than during the 1920s, until 1933–34, when it finally began to decline. Although many parents made personal sacrifices during the depression to continue their children's education, these sacrifices were difficult burdens to bear, and by 1933–34 many students were having to withdraw, some during the middle of the school year. Those unable to attend the University, but interested in pursuing an education, were encouraged to enroll in extension classes or correspondence study.

The Southern Association of Colleges and Secondary Schools was indulgent and moderate during the depression regarding accreditation. However, by 1937, with the general improvement of the times, this agency began demanding that shortcomings in programs overlooked during the depression be eliminated.

In 1937, Dr. Richard D. Foster became president of the University, with Dr. Denny retiring to become chancellor. Upon President Foster's shoulders fell the responsibility of maintaining post-depression accreditation.

The Academic Consequences of Financial Hardship

The policy of financing all extension teaching on the basis of fees collected from students led to a serious situation. Faculty members engaged in extension teaching were eager to have several large classes since the extra compensation helped to carry insurance policies, which otherwise would have lapsed, or to keep up payments on homes, for example.

One result of overextended faculty members doing full-time work on campus and carrying additional work by teaching extension classes and correspondence students was an "institutional delinquency" for the University. In 1938, the Southern Association of Colleges and Secondary Schools placed the University on its "starred" list, a warning that in some respects the institution failed to meet its standards. Being placed on the starred list was the preliminary step toward probation or expulsion.

The State Legislature met in the midst of this embarrassing situation. President Foster knew that the only cure could come from additional financial support and asked the Legislature for a $295,000 annual increase in state appropriations. The Legislature appropriated only half that amount, but it was enough to bail out the University; and the Extension Division received a fair portion of this increase.

Decline in Extension Enrollment

Enrollment in extension classes for credit fell from 1,722 in 1930–31 to 309 in 1939–40. One reason for the decrease toward the end of the decade was that, from 1938 on, campus faculty members were not allowed to teach extension classes, except in emergencies, without a corresponding decrease in their campus teaching load.

But two other circumstances contributed heavily to enrollment decline. First of all, most of those enrolled in extension classes were public school teachers. Up to 25 percent of undergraduate degree requirements could be taken in extension classes, and better salaries were paid to degreed teachers. As long as there were large groups of undergraduates teaching in the public schools, there was a lively demand for extension classes. However, the number of teachers holding degrees increased from 10 percent in 1930 until, by the mid-thirties, more than half of those employed in the public schools held at least a bachelor's degree.

Secondly, until 1935, University regulations allowed credit for six semester hours of extension work toward course requirements for the master's degree. But revised regulations stipulated that credit toward a master's degree must be completed on campus, meaning that students must either take regular course work or attend the few Saturday extension classes that were available on the University campus. This eliminated those graduate extension students who could not commute to campus on Saturdays and diminished the personal interest of graduates, who as leaders, had helped organize classes.

Consultant Service, 1936

Although the number of teachers taking extension courses declined, in 1936 the Extension Division began providing help to teachers and school officials through a Consultant Service. With assistance from College of Education faculty members and Extension Division faculty members with professional degrees in education, the Consultant Service was developed in more than forty school systems, assisting a record 4,963 teachers during 1938–39. Faculty members helped teachers build better instruction programs, select materials, and develop plans to better use local resources.

1935

W.C. Crosby establishes UA membership with National University Extension Association (NUEA).

Extension teaching, which drew heavily from the College of Education, and the Consultant Service, which also required time from these same faculty members, required that the College of Education nearly double the number of its faculty members to accommodate the Extension Division. Dr. James J. Doster, Dean of the College of Education until his death in 1942, gave full support to these two programs. After his death, the programs lost support and were taken over by the College of Education. They were curtailed during World War II, primarily because of gasoline and tire rationing. They were resumed after the war, but not up to the pre-war level.

Increase in Correspondence Study

When money became tight during the depression, people began enrolling more and more in correspondence study courses, enabling them to take credit courses without commuting to extension classes or residing on campus. For some, this was the only way they could afford to take college credit courses. Enrollment nearly doubled, jumping from 1,254 in 1929–30 to a high of 2,364 in 1937–38.

People enrolled in correspondence study courses fell into several different categories. First, there were undergraduate teachers who were working toward degrees and who completed their work during summer sessions, either at the University or another institution. Many teachers were unable to attend summer school during the depression, which encouraged correspondence study. Secondly, there were those who for economic or other reasons found it impossible to come to the campus for residence work, but who planned to come later. Thirdly, there were those who had to leave school but

1936-44

3500 ALABAMA TEACHERS ENROLLED IN IN-SERVICE TRAINING AT THE COLLEGE OF EDUCATION.

who wanted to continue study at home. These first three groups were the ones which made the correspondence study enrollment mushroom during the thirties. There were two other groups of correspondence study students: those interested in a particular subject but who did not plan to work toward a college degree, and a few campus students who, because of course conflicts, were permitted to take courses by correspondence study.

Finally, in 1941, after a number of years of previous efforts, the Extension Division succeeded in introducing supervised correspondence study at the high school level, using nationally recognized courses prepared by the University of Nebraska Extension Division. Such courses were intended to supplement limited offerings of small Alabama high schools. High school correspondence study also provided an opportunity

1936

BIRMINGHAM CENTER ESTABLISHED; MONTGOMERY CENTER ESTABLISHED.

IN 1950, THE EXTENSION NEWS BULLETIN PUBLICIZED EXPANDING SERVICES AT UNIVERSITY CENTERS, SUCH AS THIS CLASS IN OFFICE SUPERVISION.

for adults who lacked a high school diploma to take high school courses by correspondence.

Establishment of Extension Centers

Responding to the demand for late afternoon and evening classes in Alabama's more populous areas, the Extension Division established University Centers, first in Birmingham, Montgomery, and Decatur in 1936, then in Mobile in 1941. Others were organized after World War II. This represented a major outreach effort on the part of the University which flourished for a number of years.

Birmingham Center, 1936

In 1935, many people in Birmingham were unemployed, leaving the future of the children in these relief families uncertain. It was at this point that the University, through the Extension Division, seized an opportunity and established the Birmingham Center. The University had long wanted to enlarge its offerings in Birmingham but lacked funds to do so.

CCS

An architect's rendering of the proposed building for the Birmingham Center, circa 1949.

Mr. Thad Holt, state relief administrator, had access to federal money to do the work but did not wish to organize the venture himself. The University and Mr. Holt together arranged for the Extension Division to take charge of the program, using relief instructors and choosing students from relief families. Others were also allowed to enroll.

An informal program began in 1935, with classes meeting in the new Jefferson County Courthouse. In the fall of 1936, the Birmingham Center opened the doors of a University-owned building in Birmingham to formally begin its operation. Edward K. Austin was the first director.

The Birmingham Center came into being under unusual circumstances. It was organized in a depression to satisfy the needs of unemployed teachers and families in distress. This period of abnormal conditions was followed by months of preparation for what became World War II. The history of the times is reflected in the course offerings and enrollment figures of this extension center.

1936-37

Non-credit courses listed in Extension Catalog for first time; 2400 students around the state enrolled in Correspondence Courses.

During 1936–37, the first year of its operation, 145 students enrolled in the 10 courses offered at the Birmingham Center. The next year enrollment rose to 181 and then, in 1940–41, to 468. During the next school year, when the United States entered the war and many people in labor and industry were mobilized to active duty or to 48-hour work weeks, enrollment at the Birmingham Center decreased.

The Federal Government provided funds to train men and women for war-related jobs and lessened the demand for credit work which the Center had been offering. In 1940, the Emergency Engineering Program began with the purpose of refreshing and upgrading college-level engineering personnel. This service began in Birmingham in January 1941, and in Mobile in March 1941, through a cooperative arrangement between the University and the Federal Office of Education. In July 1941, Congress broadened the program to include science and management, designating the program as "Engineering, Science, and Management Defense Training."

A year later the program was redesignated Engineering, Science, and Management War Training (ESMWT), which it remained until the end of the war. The Extension Division was the University's forum for administering this program. During the peak years, 1941–42 and 1942–43, 10,000 men and women each year were trained in ESMWT classes through the Extension Division. By 1944–45 the level had dropped to 1,700.

The credit program at the Birmingham Center was a no-frills operation. It simply offered courses to students who entered with well-defined purposes in mind. Credit work was confined to the first two years of the undergraduate curriculum, except in engineering, which required only one year of residence on campus. In addition, students in their junior and

END OF 1930s

DIVISION MOVES BACK INTO CARMICHAEL HALL, HAVING OUTGROWN GRAVES OFFICES.

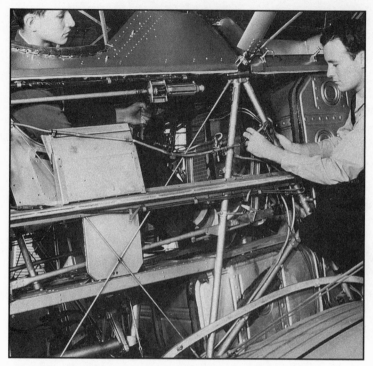

THE INCREASED INTEREST IN ENGINEERING AFTER WORLD WAR II WAS
RESPONSIBLE, IN PART, FOR THE RAPID GROWTH OF THE CENTERS.

senior years could complete as much as 25 percent of their
upper-level work through general extension classes offered at
the Center. Students were primarily interested in commerce
and business administration courses and engineering courses.

Montgomery Center, 1936

The Montgomery Center opened in the fall of 1936 at
Baldwin Junior High School with 143 students, increasing to
151 the next year. The teaching staff was composed of regular
University faculty members and faculty members from Hun-
tington College, all teaching night classes. Alex S. Pow served
as director beginning in 1947. During 1939–40, 175 students
were enrolled in 14 classes, but this was the peak of the

THE LIBRARY SERVICES PROGRAM OF THE EXTENSION DIVISION, UNDER THE LEADERSHIP OF BETHEL FITE (RIGHT), PLAYED AN IMPORTANT ROLE IN DEVELOPING THE LIBRARIES AT THE CENTERS.

THE MONTGOMERY CENTER LIBRARY, CIRCA 1947.

enrollment before the end of the war. Men were called into the armed forces and women often had jobs with irregular hours or overtime work. Enrollment dropped sharply until, in 1942–43, the four small classes that were organized had to be discontinued by the middle of the year. In 1943–44, no classes were organized at all.

Decatur Center, 1936

In 1936, an Extension Center was also started in Decatur. Enrollment that first year was only 74, dropping to 65 the second year. Because of apparent lack of interest, the Decatur Center was discontinued after the second year.

Mobile Center, 1941

In June 1941, the Mobile Center began offering evening credit courses in the historic old Barton Academy on Govern-

ERIK OVERBEY COLLECTION, UNIVERSITY OF SOUTH ALABAMA ARCHIVES

BARTON ACADEMY, MOBILE, CIRCA 1920.

1940-44

EMERGENCY WORLD WAR II TRAINING PROGRAMS.

ment Street, with administrative offices in the old Federal Building on 29 North Royal Street. From the beginning, emphasis was on engineering and commerce and business administration in anticipation of impending industrial growth and a demand for engineering and commerce graduates. Paul Brunson was the first director. In September, 1941, the city of Mobile let the University use all the space on the third floor of the old Federal Building, converting it into 17 lecture and laboratory rooms. Enrollment the first year was 158, climbing to 191 by 1943–44.

With its shipbuilding activities, Mobile experienced perhaps the greatest upsurge of industrial activity of any community in the state engaged in war industry. While the Mobile Center program emphasized credit courses for students interested in commerce and engineering, the greatest bulk of work was in organizing the federally supported ESMWT courses for men and women engaged in war work. Several thousand people were trained through the Mobile Center in this program.

NUEA Association

When Dr. Tidwell began directing the Extension Division in 1930, he became actively involved in the National University Extension Association (NUEA). W. C. Crosby, assistant director of the Extension Division until his death in 1935, had initiated NUEA membership for the University. NUEA was the most prestigious national group to which the Extension Division could belong. Many of Dr. Tidwell's ideas for extension activities came directly from his association with other universities in NUEA. He was aware of what other extension divisions were doing and drew from their experience.

1941

MOBILE CENTER ESTABLISHED.

Club Study, 1933

Although a club study service for the women's clubs of the state had been initiated by Dr. James S. Thomas, former director of the Extension Division, it was not formally organized until 1933–34. This service had been carried on incidentally during previous years by faculty members who cooperated in developing club yearbooks and special programs. In 1933, the Extension Division employed a part-time supervisor of the adult education service, which administered the club study. The supervisor also spent part of her time teaching English correspondence courses. In 1943, she began devoting full time to adult education services.

In 1935, the club study service began awarding four University scholarships to the Alabama Federation of Women's Clubs for the clubs presenting the four highest-ranked study outlines. These clubs could, in turn, present the scholarships to four outstanding high school students entering as freshmen at the University. The winning study outlines were then distributed to other clubs as examples. Although the yearly contest continued for some time, the practice of distributing winning programs was discontinued in the late 1940s. In the 1950s, the Annual Summer Workshop for the Alabama Federation of Women's Clubs, which grew out of a Youth Conservation Workshop, began to assist club program chairmen in similar ways.

Drama Loan, 1936

Begun in 1936, the drama loan service provided plays for high school teachers, church groups, and little theater groups. The publishers provided free copies, hoping that exposure to their plays would prompt orders. These plays were to be used

1943

LEGISLATURE VOTES TO PROVIDE THE UA ANNUALLY WITH FUNDS FOR THE ENCOURAGEMENT, DEVELOPMENT, AND MAINTENANCE OF RESEARCH WORK AND FOR THE FURTHER DEVELOPMENT AND SUPPORT OF THE UNIVERSITY'S EXTENSION PROGRAM.

CCS

THE DRAMA LOAN SERVICE, BEGUN IN 1936, PROVIDED PLAYS FOR READING AND
SELECTION TO HIGH SCHOOL TEACHERS, CHURCH GROUPS, AND LITTLE THEATERS
WELL INTO THE 1960S.

strictly for reading and selection, not for play rehearsals (although many groups apparently did use them for rehearsals,
as indicated by plays that were returned with annotations).

As interest in drama waned a bit in high schools, and as local
libraries offered more plays on their shelves by the mid-1960s,
requests for copies of plays began to diminish. Also, some
federal funds became available to the schools for drama
materials.

In 1939, a small rental library of current books, both fiction
and non-fiction, was created especially for small-town and
rural readers who had access to limited library facilities. This
library also fell under the auspices of the adult education
service.

1944

DR. J. R. MORTON IS NAMED DIRECTOR OF ADULT EDUCATION.

Bethel Fite

"THE EXTENSION DIVISION AT ITS BEST WAS MOTIVATED BY A BROAD VISION— THE HOPE THAT THE RESOURCES OF THE UNIVERSITY OF ALABAMA COULD BE MADE AVAILABLE TO THE ENTIRE STATE, OR TO ANYONE WITH THE INITIATIVE TO SEEK OUT WHAT WE COULD OFFER."

HOOLE SPECIAL COLLECTIONS

Library Extension and Program Services, 1946–1976

In 1946, Miss Bethel Fite was hired to head Library Extension and Program Services for the Extension Division. The principal focus of the program was to enable people who lived in towns with limited library facilities to take advantage of the materials of the University. A professionally trained librarian, Miss Fite brought expertise and enthusiasm to the post. She administered the program for 30 years.

While Library Extension and Program Services had begun as a service primarily for the Alabama Federation of Women's Clubs, in 1946 the program's focus broadened. Miss Fite made contact with people who ran smaller libraries in the state and worked with them to serve their communities with all types of materials, not just those required by the Women's Clubs. Library Extension also held training sessions and workshops for program chairmen in various kinds of clubs.

Under the guidance of Dr. Tidwell, Miss Fite worked directly with Center librarians to help the Centers in Birmingham, Montgomery, Gadsden, Mobile, and Dothan develop libraries to serve the students enrolled there.

As the Centers gained facilities, such as libraries that could serve students, they evolved toward eventual independence.

When graduate training in library service became available at The University in the early 1970s through the Graduate

School of Library Service, Miss Fite worked with Dean James B. Ramer and the library service faculty members to offer workshops for community library directors. Many of these local directors had no professional training and could thus be greatly served by continuing education seminars from library service experts on the University campus. The Alabama Library Association and Alabama Public Library Service also participated in planning and sponsoring these programs.

Typical programs on which Library Extension and Program Services and the Graduate School of Library Service combined forces from 1972–75 were: "Beyond the Library Walls: A Conference to Maximize Reference Service, Identify Information Needs, and Demonstrate Data Retrieval" in February 1972 and "Renaissance or Reformation: The Changing Content, Structure, and Process of Library Education" offered the next year. In February 1974, a conference called "Through a Glass Darkly: The Enigmatic Future of Library Education" was held in the Continuing Education Center in Tuscaloosa. In 1975, another conference pegged to "The Librarian as Educator" was mounted. These types of conferences continued for several years.

As community libraries across the state grew under better trained directors, the need for Library Extension and Program Services diminished. The program was continued for a couple of years after Miss Fite's retirement in 1976, but was eventually phased out. However, her dedication to extending the materials and resources of The University of Alabama to people throughout the state continues to serve as a model for other services today. And her influence in nurturing library service can be seen on the campuses of the former Extension Centers throughout the state.

❖❖❖

1945
CPA REVIEW COURSE INITIATED.

DOYLE BUCKLES
DIRECTED THE
UNIVERSITY NEWS
BUREAU AND SERVED
AS FIELD MANAGER OF
THE ALABAMA PRESS
ASSOCIATION FROM
1939 UNTIL HIS
DEATH IN 1947.

Alabama Press Association, 1939

In 1939, an interesting liaison began between the University News Bureau (started by President Denny in 1928) and the Alabama Press Association (APA). Large and small Alabama newspapers were having a hard time emerging from the depression years. As a group, they felt sure that the University could provide technical assistance to help them back on their feet. In 1939, the University employed Doyle Buckles, an experienced newspaperman, to serve half-time as field manager of the APA and half-time as director of the News Bureau. The arrangement worked out well, although there was some skepticism on the part of some newspapers about maintaining the integrity of a free press.

Much of the News Bureau's effort during the 1940s was spent in promoting the Extension Division, not just through

1946

GADSDEN CENTER ESTABLISHED.

the *Extension News Bulletin*, but also through news releases to local and statewide media.

Extension News Bulletin

The field manager-director of APA was directly responsible to Dr. Tidwell in the Extension Division. In addition, in 1943, he became editor of The University of Alabama *Extension News Bulletin*, which began as a four-page printed bulletin containing Extension and general University news. At first it was simply a monthly announcement of various extension activities: correspondence study courses, University center course announcements, book lists, radio broadcast schedules, club study, and drama loan service announcements. These announcements continued to alternate monthly with the news bulletin, all grouped under *Extension News Bulletin*. In 1967, the bulletin was revamped, taking a magazine format published every other month and called simply *Extension*. Publication stopped in 1969.

Redevelopment of Visual Aids, 1941

In 1941, several factors led to the redevelopment of visual aids in the Extension Division, which had been introduced in 1920 and had faded out by 1930. The 16mm sound projector had been perfected, along with nonflammable film that reduced the serious fire hazard that had accompanied motion pictures. In addition, rural electrification encouraged the use of projectors in rural schools. Film producers had collaborated with educators and educational institutions in producing films. Also, simple projection equipment that could be used in the classroom lowered the maintenance costs.

1947–48

Dr. Tidwell serves as NUEA President.

UNIVERSITY NEWS BUREAU STAFF DISCUSS A PUBLICITY RELEASE, CIRCA 1950.

The Extension Division recognized the need for a visual aids service, but funds were difficult to secure. The National Youth Administration (NYA), created after the depression, saw a work opportunity for youth and trained competent young people to work in film libraries and to assist in film production. In 1941, the NYA felt that the University should sponsor the project and gave its films and personnel to the Extension Division. Dr. James F. Caldwell became director of visual aids.

At first, in 1941–42, only 25 schools borrowed from the film library, but that number doubled by the next year. By 1944, the initial 200 films were increased to 600 films, many dealing with the war effort. In 1945–46, the Extension Division hired a photographer, beginning a production service and a file of photographs and negatives for publicity and news purposes.

By 1949–50, the Audio-Visual Aids Service booked nearly 8,000 films and had to refuse 1,500 requested bookings. In addition, it provided 9,000 identification pictures for student activity books, filmed all varsity football games, the state basketball tournament, A-Day activities, and printed more than 1,000 still photographs. In addition to campus activities, audio-visual aids provided services to women's clubs, industrial concerns, churches, and other organizations.

Speakers Bureau

Although a speakers bureau had been established at the inception of the Extension Division in 1919, no special effort was made to centrally organize speaking requests within the Extension Division. Many departments throughout the University filled requests for speakers on an individual basis. Even during the 1940s, when the Extension Division was providing a number of faculty members as speakers and forum leaders, the University was not channelling all its requests for speakers through the Division.

Radio

Early in the depression, radio station WAPI in Birmingham, jointly owned by The University of Alabama, Alabama Polytechnic Institute, and the Alabama College for Women, began having financial difficulty. In 1931, the three schools were forced to lease WAPI to commercial interests, with the stipulation that each school would have a certain allotted time to use for its own broadcasts. The University Extension Division continued to send faculty members to Birmingham for live broadcasts until about 1934, when, for lack of funds, this practice was discontinued.

Early in 1941, the University reexamined its investment in

1949

SELMA CENTER ESTABLISHED.

GRAYDON AUSMUS BECAME DIRECTOR OF RADIO BROADCASTING SERVICES WITHIN THE EXTENSION DIVISION IN 1945.

radio with the help of John Carlile, an experienced program manager formerly of CBS Radio, and a radio engineer (also from CBS). Based on their reports, the University constructed broadcasting studios in the Alabama Union Building ballroom. Construction was supervised by the CBS engineer.

The University had never fully utilized the time reserved for it on WAPI. Using telephone lines, the University began sending programs broadcast live from the new studios to WAPI to be put on the air at Birmingham. This was before the era of tape recordings and FM relays. This activity solidified in 1942 under the newly created department of Radio and Function of Broadcasting, directed by Mr. Carlile. He taught some of the first classes in broadcasting at the University, but had to leave the University in 1943 to help with radio utilization during the war.

Initially, the department of Radio and Function of Broad-

1950

HUNTSVILLE CENTER ESTABLISHED.

casting had three purposes: providing a practice studio for radio broadcasting students; producing general interest programs with the help of students and faculty members for the general listening public; and producing classroom programs to be used in the public schools.

In 1940, the student instruction division of the radio broadcasting service became the Radio Arts department of the College of Arts and Sciences. In 1945, the University employed Graydon Ausmus as the new director of broadcasting services, which had remained under the Extension Division. In 1946, the Radio Arts Department brought Leo Martin in as head and Mr. Ausmus continued as head of broadcasting. To further adult education in Alabama, the University launched FM radio station WUOA in 1949, one of the first in the nation. It remained on the air until early 1964, and after remaining silent for two years, finally returned its license to the Federal Communications Commission in 1966.

Radio station WUAL, a 10-watt station begun in 1970 and used strictly for student training, became a 100,000-watt public radio station in January 1982. Another 100-watt FM station, WVUA, was created for student training purposes.

WUAL was operated by the University Radio Services,

UNIVERSITY RADIO SPECIALISTS ASSISTING IN A COMMUNITY BROADCAST, CIRCA 1950.

created in the College of Communication to operate the public radio station. WVUA was operated by the Department of Broadcast and Film Communication, which later became Telecommunication and Film.

During the first few years after the department of Radio and Function of Broadcasting was set up in 1940, only one or two 30-minute broadcasts a week were being transmitted to WAPI. Radio station WJRD in Tuscaloosa also broadcast some University programs during this time. By 1951, eight 30-minute broadcasts were being sent out each week, not only to WAPI, but to a total of 40 radio stations, both FM and AM.

As new methods of distribution appeared, the University improved its own methods. Disc recordings were made of broadcasts and sent to stations in the mail, permitting them to use the programs at their own convenience. With the arrival of tape recordings, tape distribution was used. Finally, FM relays were used, eventually covering the entire state. The stations taped the programs off the air. In 1954, all distribution of statewide broadcasts ended.

Alabama Broadcasters Association, 1950

The Alabama Broadcasters Association (ABA) was founded in 1946 and held early meetings in Tuscaloosa on the University campus. In 1950, the ABA established its first state headquarters at the University under an arrangement similar to that of the Alabama Press Association, although the secretary's salary was paid entirely by the ABA. This relationship with the Extension Division lasted until 1968, when ABA moved to Montgomery. Later in 1973, ABA returned its headquarters to campus, this time in conjunction with the Department of Broadcast and Film Communication.

EARLY 1950s
TV BROADCASTING COURSES BEGIN.

Home and Family Life Services, 1945

Beginning in 1945, the newly organized Home and Family Life Services began operating through the Extension Division; it later developed into Home Economics Extension. The director helped people plan family-oriented programs for local areas throughout the state. In addition, she presented programs in Alabama high schools on human birth, using the Dickenson Birth Models.

Dr. Morton and Adult Education Development, 1944

In 1944, Dr. John R. Morton joined the Extension Division as director of Adult Education. With great enthusiasm, he set out to develop the University's program of adult education—institutes, conferences, and short courses for professional, business, industrial, and labor groups—part of a growing trend toward non-credit extension courses. The conference

CCS

THE PARENT-TEACHER INSTITUTE WAS BEGUN IN THE EARLY 1950s. SHOWN HERE ARE DELEGATES TO THE SUMMER 1967 SESSION.

idea had its origin in Dr. Abercrombie's and Dr. Doster's extension activities, but it was not until 1944 under John Morton's leadership that conferences began to be organized in earnest.

Although many people were not able to travel to campus at this time because of limited funds, the Extension Division anticipated a demand for these types of programs after the end of World War II, especially for updating professional groups. A few conferences were already being held on campus during the summer months when space was most available. Among these were the annual conference and workshop for lunch-room managers and the annual Parent-Teacher Institute. By 1953–54, the Extension Division was bringing 100 different groups to campus for conferences, short courses, and workshops. A total of 20,000 people participated annually in law, business, engineering, home economics, and education programs.

CHARLES ADAMS

PLANNING COMMITTEE MEMBERS AND CONFERENCE DIRECTOR CHARLES ADAMS (BOTTOM RIGHT) PREPARE FOR THE PERSONNEL MANAGEMENT CONFERENCE IN 1959.

Growth of Extension Centers—Gadsden Center, 1946; Selma Branch, 1949; Huntsville Center, 1950

After World War II, veterans were encouraged to begin or finish their education through the G.I. Bill. The University was unable to accommodate this sudden influx of new students on the main campus and encouraged students to take at least the first two years of undergraduate work at an extension center. Many of the G.I. Bill students wanted engineering or business courses, and these programs began to proliferate at the centers. The Birmingham Center and the Montgomery Center had been established in 1936 and the Mobile Center in 1941. In 1946, the Extension Division established the Gadsden Center, under the direction of Dr. Morton; in 1949, the Selma Branch of the Montgomery Center; and in 1950, the Huntsville Center, with George W. Campbell as director.

The centers experienced tremendous growth during this

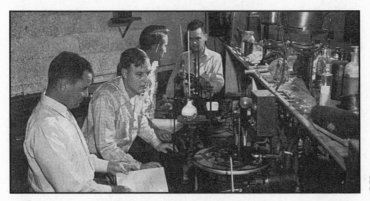

THE G.I. BILL SPURRED TREMENDOUS GROWTH AT THE EXTENSION CENTERS AFTER WORLD WAR II, ESPECIALLY IN ENGINEERING AND BUSINESS.

post-war period, thanks partially to the G.I. Bill students. During 1943–44, the lowest ebb for the centers during the war, 195 students had enrolled in Birmingham, 191 in Mobile, and none at all in Montgomery. By 1949–50, enrollments mushroomed to 2,867 students in Birmingham, 1,567 in Mobile, and 938 in Montgomery. The newer centers also boomed. By 1949–50, Gadsden had 1,603 students enrolled; Selma, in just one year, 338; and Huntsville, in only two quarters, 267. Total enrollment in extension centers that year was 7,580, compared with an on-campus enrollment of 9,058 (including the dental and medical schools in Birmingham) and an on-campus summer school enrollment of 4,738. However, by 1953–54, total extension center enrollment dropped to 4,917, reflecting the decrease in G.I. Bill students taking advantage of subsidized schooling. But thanks to the G.I. Bill students, the University extension centers became firmly established in Alabama.

BY THE END OF THE 1930s, THE EXTENSION DIVISION HAD OUTGROWN GRAVES HALL AND MOVED BACK TO CARMICHAEL HALL.

Correspondence Study—USAFI

As a direct result of World War II, the correspondence study department also received a boost. During the war, the University contracted with the United States Armed Forces Institute (USAFI) to provide correspondence study courses for soldiers stationed throughout the world. At its peak, military students comprised about 10 to 15 percent of the total correspondence study enrollment. USAFI was discontinued in 1974.

Liaison Faculty Members

During Dr. Tidwell's leadership of the Extension Division, liaison faculty members from the College of Engineering, the College of Commerce and Business Administration, the School of Home Economics, and the College of Arts and Sciences became associated with the Extension Division. They helped coordinate credit and non-credit activities between the Extension Division and the rest of the University. The Extension Division outgrew the three-office suite in Graves Hall at the end of the 1930s and moved back into Carmichael Hall, this time taking over the whole third floor of what was then the administration building.

Dr. Tidwell's Retirement, 1954

Dr. Tidwell, who had spent two and a half decades developing the Extension Division at the University, retired in 1954. Although already 70 years old, he spent the next 10 years as a presidential assistant at Stillman College in Tuscaloosa. He assisted the president by encouraging many of the teachers there to pursue additional degrees. He was able to bring in many University faculty members to serve as consultants on curriculum matters.

CHAPTER 4

ASSIMILATING LOSS AND GAIN

Era of Dr. John R. Morton, 1954–1969

B y the early 1950s, the extension efforts at the University were well in place in a number of areas. The post-war boom meant that many G.I. Bill students attended classes at the extension centers, as well as on the main campus. Further, people working in the professions, business, and industry wanted to catch up on technology, spurring growth of non-credit short courses and workshops. This was a time of rapid expansion of adult continuing education at the University.

Dr. John Morton, who had accomplished much as director of Adult Education, became the third administrator and the second dean of the Extension Division upon Dr. Tidwell's retirement in 1954. In addition to serving as dean of the Extension Division, he had initiated, through NUEA, plans with the Atomic Energy Commission during the late 1940s and early 1950s for its Museum on Atomic Energy at Oak Ridge to develop and circulate a number of mobile exhibits throughout the United States. These exhibits have been seen by thousands of students and formed the bases for a national series of seminars on atomic energy for journalists, teachers, engineers, and other groups.

Under Dr. Morton's leadership, the existing departments of the Extension Division were continued with a particular

DR. JOHN R. MORTON

strengthening of Educational Television (ETV), the off-campus resident centers, conference activities, and commerce extension services, among others.

Evidence of the demand for adult education throughout the state at this time could be seen in the popularity of the University extension centers and in the local efforts of the communities in which extension centers were located.

Around the state, communities in which extension centers were located contributed to the extension effort through capital investments or dedication of existing space for classes. The Birmingham Center erected an extension building costing $750,000. At Montgomery, the city had erected a half-million-dollar building for Extension Division use. Citizens in Mobile urged the University to offer a four-year program, furnished space in the old Federal Building to the Extension Division, and were ready to erect a million-dollar building for Univer-

---

1954

DR. JOHN R. MORTON NAMED DEAN OF EXTENSION DIVISION.

---

sity classes. Gadsden built a building which was available to the Extension Division.

The centers later grew to such an extent that some of them were destined to became autonomous institutions of higher education. Notably, the Birmingham and Huntsville centers eventually became The University of Alabama at Birmingham and the University of Alabama in Huntsville. And the Mobile and Montgomery centers evolved into free-standing institutions not affiliated with the University of Alabama: the Mobile center became the University of South Alabama and the Montgomery Center became Auburn University at Montgomery.

Dr. Morton's *University Extension in the United States*

In 1953, a year before becoming acting dean, Dr. Morton had written a report called *University Extension in the United States* as the culmination of a nationwide NUEA study. It was the first work of its kind and for many years the only reference available to extension divisions.

The following paragraph from Dr. Morton's report provides a forceful example of his passion and clarity of purpose:

> It seems obvious that, if The University of Alabama expects to engage in any program of adult education which will be of genuine service to the people who wish to take part in it, there must be worked out some procedures which do not obstruct the use and ready availability of these services. It is our belief that there is no desire on the part of anyone to compromise standards of excellence which the various schools and departments of the University may seek to establish and maintain. It seems to be plain, however, that *a very different relationship will have to exist between the University and its students where the students are adults who wish to take full responsibility for their success or failure,* and between the University and its students in cases where those students are not experienced adults and where the University is, at least to some degree, held responsible by parents for the

guidance of students who are not self-supporting and who are not of legal age.

In fact, the number of adults served by the Division greatly increased during the fifteen years of Dr. Morton's tenure. Participants in conference activities doubled, from approximately 25,000 to 50,000 people involved in conferences: from one-day meetings to seminars lasting two or three days or more, to short courses lasting several weeks, such as the annual CPA Review Course. The age of the adult student was dawning and though some of the growing pains for the Extension Division would be difficult, they were a necessary part of the process.

Educational Television, A National Leader

The University of Alabama proved to be a national leader in the area of educational television (ETV), pioneering the development of an ETV statewide network and providing leader-

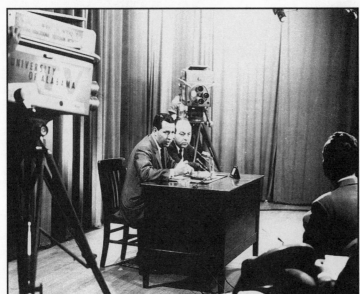

NATIONALLY KNOWN BROADCASTER DOUGLAS EDWARDS IS SHOWN HERE IN THE UNIVERSITY EDUCATIONAL TELEVISION STUDIO, CIRCA 1960.

JUDY HOSKINS PORTRAYED AGNES IN UNIVERSITY TELEVISION'S "BEAUTY AND THE LONELY BEAST," A CHILDREN'S PLAY PRODUCED IN 1969.

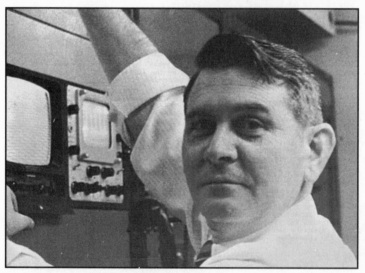

JOE STUCKY, ETV CENTER CHIEF ENGINEER, OVERSAW OPERATIONS FOR THE NATIONAL HOOK-UP WITH NET BEGINNING IN 1969.

ship for other developing stations. The University demonstrated its commitment by building state-of-the-art television studios patterned after a major network's (CBS). In addition, in the late 1950s, the University's ETV station was the first television station in Alabama (including commercial stations) to purchase an Ampex 2-inch quad videotape machine. The advent of videotape meant superior output and allowed the University to relay programs in much better quality to other stations across the state.

Although the groundwork was being laid before Dr. Tidwell retired, it was not until November 1955 that the University began broadcasting educational television under the auspices of the Extension Division. University president John M. Gallalee, encouraged by Dr. Tidwell, had reserved a television channel with the Federal Communications Commission (FCC) for the University. In 1951, the FCC had pledged to hold a number of television channels for educational television for two years before allowing them to become commercial channels.

Only two groups in Alabama were awarded VHF channels—The University of Alabama and the Greater Birmingham Area ETV Commission. Others that applied, including Alabama Polytechnic Institute (Auburn University), were allocated UHF channels, which at that time were virtually useless since most TV sets could not receive UHF signals.

Alabama governor Gordon Persons, who was a radio buff and also interested in ETV, readily saw the value of a state-wide ETV network and formed the Alabama Educational Television Commission. He was able to channel a half-million excess dollars from the State Docks to the ETV network, which put it on its feet financially. The only two VHF channels allocated in Alabama—Channel 7 to the University and Channel 10 to Birmingham—were in close proximity. University president O. C. Carmichael (who succeeded President Gallalee in 1953) permitted Channel 7 to be removed to Mt. Cheaha in east-central Alabama, the highest point in the state, with the condition that the University would have equal time access to the network from campus studios. He also stipulated that Channel 7 would revert to the University if the network failed.

Even though the transmitter for the University's channel had been relocated, The University of Alabama provided the leadership for the Alabama ETV network. Channel 7 itself went on the air in early fall 1955 and became the ninth ETV channel in the United States to begin broadcasting. The University television station began operating in November 1955. Channel 10 in Birmingham was the tenth ETV station to go on the air. Both channels were awarded $10,000 by the General Electric Corporation for being among the first ten ETV channels in the nation to begin broadcasting.

In addition, the Ford Foundation granted $10,000 to The University of Alabama for a third camera, a slide-film chain, and a "kinescope recorder" (the forerunner of the video-tape recorder). In exchange for the grant, the University agreed to become affiliated with the National Educational Television and Radio Center (NET), a programming agency funded by the Ford Foundation. This affiliation was highly desirable for the University, which could then draw from the NET programs, as the University functioned as the programming center for the Alabama ETV network.

The University maintained NET affiliation until July 1, 1969, when the affiliation was assumed by the Alabama ETV Commission. After that, some controversy arose over the editing out of any potentially controversial programs, especially black-oriented programs, and the FCC reversed its decision to renew the Alabama ETV network station licenses in 1971. The Alabama ETV network continued to operate, but became ineligible for federal funds.

The University of Alabama, Alabama Polytechnic Institute, and the Greater Birmingham Area ETV Commission shared time on the Alabama ETV network, which was on the air in the afternoons and evenings, Monday through Friday, for many years. The three agencies jointly carried out the scheduling and program-planning, each having equal prime and non-prime time. Time slots could be traded to suit the needs of the different agencies. Later, additional production studies were added throughout the state to furnish programming for the network.

The University decided to use ETV for the development of in-school programs, while Alabama Polytechnic Institute used ETV strictly for adult education. They exchanged time slots so that the University could have more daytime exposure and Alabama Polytechnic Institute could have more evening exposure.

In 1956, a Ford Foundation grant of $400,000, utilized jointly by the University, Alabama Polytechnic Institute, and the Greater Birmingham Area ETV Commission, helped develop ETV use in Alabama's classrooms over a three-year period. With this grant, the three agencies arranged workshops and conferences for teachers and administrators to learn effective use of ETV and to help arrange classroom programming to fit into their teaching schedules.

The development of ETV, and nurturing of what eventually became University Television Services, under the auspices of the Extension Division was an important means of extending educational resources to countless citizens directly into their homes or classrooms. University Television Services became a functioning program in the University's School of Public Communication (later the College of Communication) in the fall of 1973.

Alabama Press Association
Relationship Dissolved, 1956

In 1956, the Alabama Press Association (APA) and the

1955

UA BECOMES NATIONAL LEADER IN EDUCATIONAL TELEVISION. FIRST ETV BROADCASTS FROM UNIVERSITY TELEVISION STUDIOS IN NOVEMBER 1955.

THE EXTENSION DIVISION MOVED TO MANLY HALL IN 1955.

News Bureau, which had been sharing a half-time secretary-director, dissolved their relationship. At that time the News Bureau employed its first full-time director. However, there remained a close relationship between the News Bureau and the APA since they shared adjacent rooms in Manly Hall. (The Extension Division had moved its offices from Carmichael Hall to Manly Hall in September 1955).

In January 1969, administrative control for APA moved from the Extension Division to the Journalism Department. After the News Bureau moved from Manly Hall into the new Rose Administration Building that same year, the relationship between the APA and the News Bureau concluded. In August 1973, the APA moved off campus to downtown Tuscaloosa.

Continuing Legal Education

Continuing Legal Education was organized in 1960 through the support of the Alabama Bar Association, which contributed several thousand dollars each year. Cumberland

School of Law at Samford University also contributed to program. Although this program was initially organized under the Extension Division, in 1973 it was moved to the Law School and remained a separate continuing education program.

Tuscaloosa Evening Classes

In the fall of 1955, the Extension Division began offering evening classes on the main University campus for residents of Tuscaloosa and surrounding communities. Initially, 11 credit courses and three non-credit courses were taught, with a total of 173 students enrolled during 1955–56.

The evening classes grew for several years, enrolling 180 credit students and 173 non-credit students in 1958-59. But in 1959-60, credit enrollments dropped to 128 and non-credit enrollments increased to 186. Partially because of the difficulty in projecting how many people might be interested in taking evening courses, evening classes were discontinued in 1962.

Evolution of the Extension Centers, 1956–1969

From 1956-69, as community needs shifted and junior colleges across the state opened their doors, the extension centers of The University of Alabama underwent major changes. All extension centers except one—the Gadsden Center—eventually left the University; changes at the centers were unique to each location. Another important organizational change occurred in 1975 with the creation of The University of Alabama System. The system formalized the Huntsville and Birmingham campuses as free-standing, degree-granting institutions and co-campuses with The University of Alabama's main campus in Tuscaloosa.

1955

EXTENSION DIVISION MOVES TO MANLY HALL.

In addition to extension centers in Birmingham, Mobile, Gadsden, Huntsville, and Montgomery (with its Selma branch), the Extension Division opened another center in Dothan in 1956.

Shortly after the Dothan Center was established, Troy State University began offering courses at nearby Fort Rucker, giving students a chance to take a four-year program there. The Dothan Center offered only two years in most majors and thus was not able to grant degrees. Students had to transfer for their upper-level courses. In 1965, when George C. Wallace State Junior College opened in Dothan, there was less need for the Dothan Center. In 1965, the Montgomery Center took over operation of the Dothan Center, and two years later it was phased out completely.

The advent of state-supported junior colleges in Alabama in 1964 and 1965 increased the number of students statewide who began taking lower-level college courses. The junior colleges had an "open door" admissions policy and a low entrance fee and thus attracted students more readily than the University extension centers. The University remained firm in the decision not to grant degrees at the centers (although there had been the previous exception of degrees granted in engineering at the Birmingham Center during World War II). Graduate courses were offered through the centers, but the University limited to 12 the number of credit hours that could be taken off-campus.

In Mobile there was a growing demand for a four-year, degree-conferring institution. Local leaders persuaded the State Legislature to fund a new school, the University of South Alabama in Mobile. In 1964, the Mobile Center was phased out, with former center director Dr. Fred Whiddon becoming the president of the new University of South Alabama.

1956

DOTHAN CENTER ESTABLISHED.

In 1965, the Huntsville Center was the next to leave the University Extension Division. However, it retained ties with the University, designating itself the University of Alabama in Huntsville. Clyde Reeves became vice-president at Huntsville under Dr. Frank Rose, who had become president of The University of Alabama in 1958.

In 1966, the Birmingham Center left the Extension Division, becoming the University of Alabama at Birmingham with Dr. Joseph Volker as vice-president under President Rose. President Rose retired in 1969 and Dr. David Mathews became president of The University of Alabama (main campus). The same year Dr. Volker became president at Birmingham, and Dr. Benjamin Graves became president at Huntsville. The relationship between these two offspring of the University and their parent remained close. In 1975, The University of Alabama System was created by the Board of Trustees. All three campuses—Tuscaloosa, Huntsville, and Birmingham—were thus joined. Dr. Volker became the first chancellor of the System in 1976 and served until 1981.

People in Montgomery also wanted the University to establish a four-year school there, similar to those at Huntsville and Birmingham. However, President Rose felt that the University shouldn't undertake additional building projects. So in 1968, in an agreement between Dr. Rose and Auburn University president Dr. Harry Philpott, the Montgomery Center and the Selma branch were given to Auburn University.

By 1968, all extension centers of the University except the Gadsden Center were free-standing entities and no longer affiliated with the Extension Division. When Gadsden State Junior College was opened, there was some thought of also closing the Gadsden Center.

However, perceptive city leaders in Gadsden knew there was a need for educational opportunities beyond the two-year

---

1958-59

Dr. Morton serves as NUEA President.

---

level, so through negotiations with University officials they kept the Center open. This good working relationship facilitated the blossoming of the Gadsden program throughout the 1970s and into the 1980s and 1990s.

* * *

The extension centers of The University of Alabama served a tremendously important purpose statewide for some thirty years: extending the resources of the main campus to a vast constituency of people in Alabama. As educational needs changed throughout the state and as a variety of forces— economics, community needs, even politics—came to bear, the centers evolved into institutions apart from the main campus. Though it might appear that the University's extended circle of learners was diminishing, in fact, a simultaneous gearing-up of conference activities on the main campus during this time provided many new constituencies with access to the University's resources. Innovative programs and delivery methods paved the way for the development of a highly various and sophisticated continuing education effort at the University that would begin in the late sixties and continue evolving to the present day.

Conference Activities, 1956-1968

In 1956, the Extension Division employed Mr. Charles Adams as its first coordinator of conference activities, an area that had grown considerably during the previous decade. Until that time, the liaison for each conference also had to arrange for logistics such as reserving meeting rooms, planning meals, and the other details of conference management,

---

1960

CONTINUING LEGAL EDUCATION ORGANIZED.

Charles Adams

"IN OUR DIVISION'S HEYDAY, WE HANDLED 200–250 PROGRAMS PER YEAR. WE CONCENTRATED ON MAKING ALL ASPECTS OF THE PROGRAMS RUN SMOOTHLY. THIS INVOLVED A LOT OF PROBLEM-SOLVING."

in addition to program planning. But after 1956, such details were arranged by the conference activities coordinator, thus making for a more organized and businesslike operation within the Extension Division.

In the fall of 1956, fewer than 20 conferences, workshops, or other non-credit programs were offered. Some of these included: Alabama Bankers, the Alabama Press Association, the tax clinic and human resources management conferences, and a probation and parole officers conference.

At this point, the division had a liaison with each major college of the University, and each academic unit had its own program development representative for the area. These representatives each had an academic appointment and some taught one or two courses per term. At this time, when a program was planned, three components were involved: the Extension Division provided resources and know-how to facilitate the activity; the academic unit provided faculty; and a representative from the clientele provided networking within the appropriate constituency.

1964

MOBILE EXTENSION CENTER BECOMES THE UNIVERSITY OF SOUTH ALABAMA.

As the Extension Division staff in the 1950s sought to solve problems of continuing education using resources of the University, industry, and the private sector, there was also a very real need to put together the nuts and bolts of conference management.

Mr. Adams and his staff were involved in creating a system of accounting; appropriate packaging such as name tags, packets, parking permits, and acknowledgement letters; and creating graphic identifier elements for the Division, among other things, for Conference Activities. As conference coordinator, Mr. Adams oversaw all the details necessary to ensure that participation in programs went as smoothly as possible.

Among the events or programs of note with which Conference Activities were involved in the mid-1960s were the inauguration of Dr. Frank Rose as University President and the Headstart Program. When Lady Bird Johnson, President Johnson's wife, visited the campus in 1966 to review Alabama's model program and speak at the "Women and the Changing Community" conference, Mr. Adams' staff worked diligently behind the scenes registering conferees and attending to other conference details.

Review of Conference Activities Growth

In 1954-55, a total of 26,000 people were served by conferences or workshops through the Extension Division. Of these, an estimated 15,000 were involved in off-campus family-life conferences sponsored by Home Economics Extension. Another 5,000 were high school students involved in the journalism clinic, band and choral contests, and science academies coordinated by High School Services.

In the mid-sixties, conference activities continued to grow

1964-65

ADVENT OF JUNIOR COLLEGES IN ALABAMA HAS MAJOR IMPACT ON EXTENSION STATEWIDE.

CCS

In 1970, Audio-Visual Services became Educational Media, a free-standing department reporting to Academic Affairs, in order to more fully serve the University.

and by 1964–65, 6,000 adults were involved in on-campus conferences. A total of 45,000 people were being served by conference activities; 16,000 of these were high school students, an estimated 16,000 were involved in family-life conferences around the state, and 7,000 were coordinated through University centers in Birmingham and Huntsville.

Mid-1960s

As Centers become independent institutions, the Division concentrates on growth of conference activities.

In 1967-68, a total of 38,000 people were involved in conference activities. Of these, 26,000 were now involved in on-campus activities. An additional 8,000 were high school students, and an estimated 4,000 were involved in family-life conferences. In just four years, the number of adults attending conferences on-campus had more than tripled. This represents a major turning point in the Extension Division's focus — away from satellite centers of learning around the state to campus-oriented activities. And the increased emphasis on on-campus activity set the stage for a facility dedicated to continuing education administration and meetings.

Some of the conferences that developed in the 1960s were annual affairs and others were more specialized, meeting the needs of certain groups of people. During the 1960s, there was a great demand for data processing conferences to upgrade employees working in that area. Many workers had been trained on the job and lacked formal instruction. In the early years of these conferences, as many as 300 people attended. But as the data processors became experts themselves, attendance dropped.

Another specialized area involved tailor-made programs for the National Aeronautics and Space Administration (NASA) at Marshall Space Flight Center in Huntsville. Engineering extension sponsored a number of these programs between 1965 and 1967 and one in 1971.

Many of the conferences drew on outside experts as major speakers and instructors, although University faculty members participated in many of them. Often conference participants were experts themselves, which necessitated having regionally or nationally recognized experts address the group.

The model for conference management, organization, and program planning developed by Mr. Adams and other Extension Division staff continued to serve the Extension Division, and later the College of Continuing Studies, very well with modifications and evolutions taking place in the normal course of growth of non-credit activities.

MRS. LADY BIRD JOHNSON VISITED THE UNIVERSITY IN 1966 AT THE INVITATION OF PRESIDENT FRANK ROSE.

MRS. JOHNSON TOURED THE CHILD DEVELOPMENT CENTER DURING HER VISIT TO CAMPUS.

ASSIMILATING LOSS AND GAIN / 73

Project Head Start at UA Becomes National Model

During the mid-1960s, President Lyndon Johnson began promoting Project Head Start, a program designed to give preschoolers, particularly those from poor homes, background enrichment before they started their formal education. NUEA took on the task of training Head Start teachers, and the University Extension Division, as a member of NUEA, held its first training workshops in the summer of 1965. Over 1,700 people participated in workshops on the main campus and at the Huntsville, Birmingham, and Montgomery centers. The majority of the approximately 600 people who came to the University campus were black, the first large predominantly black group to be involved in an educational project on campus. Although the campus had been desegregated since 1963, the area was still racially sensitive. Many blacks were reluctant to register more than their names. However, a black student helped Mr. Adam's staff with registration and was able to gain the confidence of attendees. This program, which continued in an evolved form as the Child Development Associate Training Program, opened the door to serving blacks on campus.

It is important to note that The University of Alabama's program was used as a national model for the Head Start Program. Mrs. Lyndon Johnson invited University president Dr. Rose to the White House twice to discuss Head Start. After his second visit, Dr. Rose reciprocated with an invitation to Mrs. Johnson to visit the University campus, to speak at the "Women and the Changing Community" conference in 1966. Mrs. Johnson visited the Child Development Laboratory, run by what was then the School of Home Economics, where she met Head Start children and teachers.

1965

TITLE I FUNDS CREATED WITHIN THE HIGHER EDUCATION ACT UNDER PRESIDENT LYNDON JOHNSON.

CPA Review

Another extension activity that represented professional updating was the Certified Public Accountant (CPA) review course, which became nationally recognized. Started in 1945 by the School of Commerce and Business Administration with only a handful of participants, it was the forerunner of in-depth professional review courses around the country. In a 1963 study, 75 percent of those responding to the questionnaire who had taken the CPA review course at the University said they had passed the CPA exam and were issued certificates by their respective state boards of accountancy. At that time, the University was able to accommodate about 72 people during each of the two sessions the course was offered (one in fall and one in spring). Because of long waiting lists, for a few summers during the 1960s an additional summer session was offered. This program continues to thrive in 1992, with enrollments averaging about 50 participants during each of the two sessions.

Civil Defense Training

At the time the Montgomery Center was given to Auburn, the University decided to continue to maintain a Montgomery Office of Research and Services. Several programs were administered through this office, one of which was the Civil Defense Training program.

Begun in 1963, the Alabama Department of Civil Defense contracted with the University to provide civil defense training to city and county officials. The program itself was initiated nationally through NUEA. Administered through the Extension Division, it was at first geared toward preparing for

---

1965

HUNTSVILLE EXTENSION CENTER BECOMES THE UNIVERSITY OF ALABAMA IN HUNTSVILLE. CLYDE REEVES IS VICE-PRESIDENT AT HUNTSVILLE, UNDER DR. FRANK ROSE. LATER, IN 1969, DR. BENJAMIN GRAVES IS NAMED PRESIDENT OF UAH.

---

nuclear disaster—especially since the 1962 Cuban Missile Crisis had presented a real threat of such a disaster. After 1970, emphasis shifted more to preparing for natural disasters, and the program was renamed "Emergency Preparedness."

Title I Funds

Title I, created by the Higher Education Act of 1965 under President Lyndon Johnson, was administered through the Montgomery Office. Title I funds provided for a government employees' extension service throughout the United States, similar to the farm extension, to improve government service. In addition, the Title I funds provided for training in health areas and for assistance to small businesses. NUEA was instrumental in securing this funding from Congress.

Col. Robert W. Springfield, who joined the University Extension Division as director of the Montgomery Center in 1963, became director of Title I funds for the State of Alabama after the Higher Education Act of 1965 was passed. Although the University and Auburn University shared joint control of distribution of funds, Col. Springfield and The University of Alabama acted as the agent for the state in distributing funds. When the Montgomery Center was turned over to Auburn, he remained in the Montgomery Office of Research and Services. William Jones took over as director in fall 1977 after Col. Springfield retired. The Montgomery office then began functioning as the Montgomery Regional Office, reporting directly to the UA President. Although Title I remains authorized, dollars ceased to be available through the program in 1980.

Municipal Training Institute for City Clerks

The first program that the Extension Division established with Title I funds was the Municipal Training Institute for City Clerks in 1966. Under Title I arrangements, the University provided two-thirds of the cost of such programs from

Title I funds and the municipalities provided one-third. Since 1970, several municipal-employees groups that were already established have enlisted Title I aid through the University, and a half-dozen new groups have been established with Title I aid.

Col. Robert W. Springfield

COL. ROBERT W. SPRINGFIELD

"AFTER MY MILITARY CAREER, THE UNIVERSITY OF ALABAMA GAVE ME A CHANCE TO CONTINUE MY GREAT LOVE, WHICH WAS EDUCATION AT EVERY LEVEL. I THOROUGHLY ENJOYED WORKING WITH ADULTS, HELPING COUNSEL THEM AND FURTHER THEIR EDUCATION."

In 1963, Col. Robert W. Springfield was named director of The University of Alabama's Montgomery Center. Col. Springfield took over the struggling center that had been formed initially to serve military personnel at Maxwell Air Force Base. In his second year on the job he was named assistant dean of Continuing Education. Because Dean Morton was at that time in poor health and often unable to travel and attend meetings, Col. Springfield frequently served in an acting dean capacity.

In addition to his duties as director of the Montgomery Center, Col. Springfield also administered the Selma Center and shared some of the responsibility for the Gadsden and Dothan Centers.

After Auburn took over the Montgomery Center in 1967, Col. Springfield became involved in the upgrade of the recently acquired conference and retreat facility, Ann Jordan Lodge in Coosa County. Col. Springfield personally supervised crews building the new lodging at Ann Jordan.

In 1967, when Montgomery became the headquarters for a number of Title I programs, Auburn University and The University of Alabama joined forces on these programs. Four deans and one vice president from each institution sat on a board chaired by Col. Springfield. Col. Springfield handled the fiscal aspects of the programs, including writing proposals for federal funds and receiving proposals for projects from institutions in the state of Alabama.

Outstanding Title I programs were those in the areas of municipal employee training, small business training, and healthcare. Institutions around the state that participated and received Title I funding included Auburn University, Troy State University, Spring Hill College, the University of Alabama at Birmingham, Tuskegee University, Calhoun Junior College, and other colleges and junior colleges.

Col. Springfield conducted Head Start classes for teachers at the Montgomery Center during the time of the civil rights march from Selma to Montgomery. Blacks attending the integrated classes were housed and fed in Montgomery without incident or threat to their safety.

Col. Springfield retired from the University in 1977 and was named assistant dean emeritus. The Board of Trustees recognized him with a proclamation commending his contribution to the growth of Adult Education in the State of Alabama.

1966

Birmingham Extension Center becomes University of Alabama at Birmingham with Dr. Joseph Volker serving as first president.

Continuing Education Services
for Business and Industry

Another program supported in part by Title I funding was Continuing Education Services for Business and Industry, started in 1966, with headquarters in Gadsden. Available primarily for economically depressed businesses in north Alabama counties, where many small businesses were experiencing bankruptcies, Continuing Education Services for Business and Industry programs were co-sponsored by the University and local chambers of commerce. Many of the programs dealt with the clarification of such acts as the United States Truth in Lending Act and the Alabama Fair Credit Reporting Act. In addition, a tax clinic helped business people with income tax forms. In 1971, Continuing Education Services for Business and Industry began offering courses to help industries meet the requirements of the Industrial Occupational Safety and Health Act of 1970 (OSHA). Many of the programs were specifically tailored for one particular business, at its request, and held on-site.

Dr. Morton's Retirement

Dr. Morton retired from the University in 1969. During his tenure as dean, a number of important changes had taken place within the Division, including the evolution of all the extension centers, except the Gadsden Center, away from the University and the development of conference activities. The work accomplished during this time helped lay the groundwork for future developments as the Extension Division grew toward becoming a division of continuing education.

1968

MONTGOMERY CENTER, INCLUDING THE SELMA BRANCH, THROUGH AN AGREEMENT BETWEEN THE TWO UNIVERSITIES, BECOMES AUBURN UNIVERSITY IN MONTGOMERY. DOTHAN BRANCH IS ALSO PHASED OUT. MONTGOMERY OFFICE OF RESEARCH AND SERVICES IS ESTABLISHED, REPORTING TO THE UA PRESIDENT'S OFFICE.

PART II

MODERNIZATION OF
EXTENDED SERVICES
AND CONTINUING
EDUCATION

1969–1992

CHAPTER 5

BLUEPRINT FOR CHANGE

Era of Dr. Galen N. Drewry, 1969–1975

"ONE OF MY CENTRAL IDEALS WAS TO INSPIRE ALL OF THE EMPLOYEES OF EXTENDED SERVICES TO WORK IN HARMONY, WITH EACH INDIVIDUAL'S TALENTS MAXIMIZED AS WE GREW."

DR. GALEN N. DREWERY

I n the summer and fall of 1969, Dr. John Morton made preparations for the orderly transition of continuing education programs and activities to a successor. Late in 1969, Dr. Galen N. Drewry came to The University of Alabama's Office for Academic Affairs from the University of Georgia, where he had directed its Institute of Higher Education. Dr. Drewry was named special university consultant on Extended Educational Services and later was appointed associate academic vice-president and dean of Extended Services at UA.

Dr. Drewry had also been tapped to head the off-campus programs and would possibly oversee the conferences and short courses administration as well. Under Dr. Drewry's leadership a blueprint for the next evolutionary phase of continuing education on the University campus would be conceived.

Shortly after his arrival on campus, Dr. Drewry met with Dr. C. T. Moore, assistant vice-president on Programs and Planning with the Office for Academic Affairs, to discuss the future of Extension at The University of Alabama.

Dr. Drewry Outlines His Vision to UA Administration

In a memo to the Office for Academic Affairs dated October 17, 1969, Dr. Drewry outlined his vision for extended educational services at The University of Alabama.

Drewry proposed that a "major undertaking of the faculties and administration over the next five years must be to develop the extended instruction, research, and service components of their campus responsibilities." This could be done, Drewry wrote, "through 1) continuing education programs; 2) inter-institutional programs and agreements with junior colleges, colleges, and other universities; and 3) programmatic relationships with the appropriate governmental, educational, industrial, agricultural, legal and other social groupings.

"To accomplish such ends, extended (off-campus) educational efforts must become a constituent and substantive part of departmental and divisional education planning and development, and funding must be secured from multiple 'outside'

1969

DR. GALEN N. DREWRY COMES TO UA FROM THE UNIVERSITY OF GEORGIA TO SERVE AS SPECIAL UNIVERSITY CONSULTANT ON EXTENDED UNIVERSITY SERVICES AND IS SOON NAMED ASSOCIATE ACADEMIC VICE-PRESIDENT AND DEAN OF EXTENDED SERVICES.

---

sources as well as directly through the University budget," he proposed.

Drewry went on to emphasize the need to "modernize programs, with a much stronger emphasis on the concept of continuing education." He articulated the concept of continuing education as "a program of organized experiences growing out of needs, problems, and interests of people.

"That *learning is a life-long process*," Dr. Drewry posited, "is more than a cliche, and it proceeds best when it occurs as a systematic and continuous process from a basis of undergraduate or graduate education. The objectives of continuing education are varied: new knowledge, understanding, and techniques for use in one's work; improved ways of solving personal and public problems; general cultural growth. There must be both motivation and opportunity for an adult to learn through periodic study, whether he is a high school dropout or holds a graduate degree. To that end, continuing education is dedicated."

Dr. Drewry underscored the connection between the University's dedication to public service and the possibilities of extension and continuing education. He emphasized the need for a collegiate continuing education staff, sometimes working in cooperation with other institutions to coordinate activities. With this definition, Dr. Drewry laid the groundwork for the modern-day College of Continuing Studies model which would be led by ". . . a higher education staff with a broad concept of mission [that] can provide the thrust through which the University extends its services cooperatively with other institutions to segments of the populations not ordinarily served directly by the University."

Dr. Drewry's memo also included a well-reasoned plea for a dedicated facility for continuing education on campus, not-

1969

SOUL CITY PROJECT INITIATED THROUGH CONTINUING EDUCATION IN HOME ECONOMICS.

ing that "an attractive and comfortable facility enhances the many learning activities involved in a comprehensive continuing education program." He cited the Kellogg centers for continuing education around the country as "good models of desirable facilities."

Drewry suggested that a long-range, ten-year plan be developed for continuing education and that this plan be revised and updated annually. He closed his memo with a series of questions for the Office for Academic Affairs to consider:

1. *What significant gaps are there in the present public services and continuing education programs of the University?*
2. *What additional resources are needed to mount a comprehensive service program?*
3. *How can the University best staff for services?*
4. *Are new or additional structures needed for implementation of a comprehensive program of University services?*
5. *What sources or combinations of sources of financial support are most desirable for the service program?*

These questions set the stage for further discussion of development of the Division and led to a revised planning document for continuing education through the 1970s and into the early 1980s. The Division was at a crossroads in its evolution in 1969–70, and Dr. Drewry's foresight set the tone for the evolution of continuing education on the University campus in future years.

Dr. DrewryProposes Expansion of Services and Programs; and Strengthening the Continuing Education Unit

In a 1970–71 document called "Expanding the Service Programs of the University of Alabama," an ambitious plan for expanding the services provided by the Division and for centralizing the various continuing education units into one well-oiled machine, was put forth.

This document once again underscored Dr. Drewry's drive to lay the groundwork for a revitalized extended services and continuing education effort at The University of Alabama. He proposed that new services be undertaken and that old services be increased. Heading the list of items proposed was the Center for Continuing Education and Alumni Affairs, which, Dr. Drewry wrote, "should be one of the major undertakings of the University in expanding services in the next few years." Along with this, a telecommunications center was proposed that would "promote significant developments of educational television and other extended services utilizing telecommunications media." It would be a number of years before this dream could be fully realized in a program such as QUEST (Quality University Extended Site Telecourses), begun in 1991 at the initiation of Dean John C. Snider.

Dr. Drewry cited the need for nonresidential degree programs designed for adults and named national and international initiatives that set precedents for a such a program. He also expressed the need to develop more non-credit courses and activities, some of which might be general educational or personal development courses and others relating to occupational or community needs. He suggested that these might take place around the state as the market warranted.

A plan for four or five University field representatives in strategic locations throughout the state was proposed. In Drewry's proposal, field representatives might be employed part-time and perform a variety of services including assisting with conferences in the area, monitoring independent study exams, and providing information to the community about the University. This plan, in a revised form, did later catch the attention of President Mathews, though not in the form that Dr. Drewry had originally envisioned.

Other services he proposed included establishing a

Speaker's Bureau, publishing Extended Service Bulletins (modeled on the Agricultural Extension Service publications), providing assistance to the "undereducated" citizens of Alabama (Soul City and Head Start were models for this), and operating a counseling and guidance service for women aimed at the middle-aged homemaker seeking education for a new career. Dr. Drewry also saw that special training for employee groups was "a fruitful area for expansion," noting that programs would be offered away from the campus and would be self-supporting except for administration. Indeed, "contract" or "tailor-made" training did grow, and in the 1980s and 1990s, became a source of low-overhead, reliable income for the Division.

Enhancement of evening courses, as part of the regular residence program, was tapped as a priority for the University with convincing documentation of the difficulty that working professionals faced in getting an advanced degree at that time. Evening courses had been offered at the University since the early 1950s in various programs, but working adults still could not pursue a degree by taking courses exclusively in the evening hours.

Other community-based services that Dr. Drewry proposed were an Institute for Community Services and a Bureau of Performing Arts. He noted specific areas relating to continuing education that would be of national concern which the Division might study.

Finally, Dr. Drewry articulated the need to clarify University policies and procedures affecting Extended Services and to assign faculty resources on a released time basis for participation in Extended Services. Dr. Drewry saw the value of centralizing the division's activities and attached an excerpt from "Guidelines for Developing a Comprehensive Univer-

---

1970

DR. DREWRY ARTICULATES NEED FOR LONG-RANGE PLAN FOR CONTINUING EDUCATION'S GROWTH; PROPOSES EXPANSION OF SERVICES AND PROGRAMS.

University students assisted in the Soul City Project, teaching community members to improve homemaking skills.

sity Extension Educational Program in NASULGC Member Institutions" as a template for properly organizing a continuing education unit.

While some of the proposals that Dr. Drewry outlined in the document were begun during his tenure as dean, some took many years to reach fruition.

Soul City Project

In June 1969, the Soul City Project was initiated under the direction of Dr. Mary Catherine Beasley, Continuing Education in Home Economics. The project was funded by the U.S. Office of Education, Department of Health, Education, and Welfare (HEW) through the Adult Education Act of 1966 and it continued into the early 1970s. According to an abstract of the project from 1970, its main thrust was "to pool the combined services of several agencies of federal, state, and local governments, resources of The University of Alabama, and volunteers in order to render service to the community." Ultimately, project organizers hoped to interrupt a cycle of poverty by motivating and educating adults in a low-income area of Tuscaloosa.

Dr. Beasley and other leaders of the project strove to reach illiterate women and motivate them toward adult basic education goals through programs that would support and strengthen family life. Through a "demonstration project" approach, practical solutions to some of the problems which frequently accompany the condition of poverty were addressed. Classes in basic communication skills as well as in sewing, cooking, and purchasing were taught. Recreation programs for children, teenagers, and adults were also developed.

The headquarters for Soul City were in the Community Living-Learning Center in the Belcher's Quarters area of Tuscaloosa. In a one-mile-square area, which included the Center, there was a high concentration of low-income families and 46.8 percent of the city's substandard housing units. Disease, crime, and chronic unemployment characterized the area, according to a 1971 University News Bureau release.

While the ideal that motivated the organizers of Soul City was lofty—i.e., to help poverty-stricken community members improve their daily lives and become more productive members of society—the implementation was based entirely in programs geared toward improving practical life skills. During 1971, projects included developing 4-H Clubs, a community health survey, first aid and home nursing classes, a County Home Extension program, and cultural programs in cooperation with the Public Library Division of Alabama.

A newsletter called *The Soul City Bulletin* was published and included information about historic black figures in American culture alongside practical life information.

1970

INSTITUTE FOR HIGHER EDUCATION AND RESEARCH (IHERS) ESTABLISHED.

One encouraging gain assessed by the leaders of the project included emergence of leadership qualities in some of the Soul City residents and further involvement of the "urban black" in Adult Basic Education programs.

The Institute of Higher Education Research and Services

An initiative that Dr. Drewry personally launched was the Institute for Higher Education and Research (IHERS). As post-secondary education in Alabama and the Southeast underwent dramatic changes in the early 1970s, The University of Alabama answered the call for what President Mathews called "new and supportive responses" on the part of the University. In May 1970, Dr. Drewry announced the establishment of the Institute of Higher Education Research and Services to give identity and continuity to its efforts to aid the development of post-secondary education in Alabama.

According to a University News Bureau press statement on May 30, 1970, "the new Institute, along with other changes, will provide a major thrust in higher education programs of the University. The Institute will incorporate and expand activities now conducted by the Office of Cooperative Programs in Higher Education and will be a division of the total extended services program of the University."

Dr. Drewry brought Dr. Thomas J. Diener to campus from the University of Georgia to direct IHERS. Dr. Diener had served as professor of higher education and head of the University of Georgia's Institute of Higher Education. Among Dr. Diener's varied experience was work with the American Association of Junior Colleges and its program with developing institutions. He brought tremendous energy and enthusiasm to the University project. Dr. Diener's and Dr. Drewry's collaborative vision for IHERS resulted in a number of significant initiatives that improved the quality of research in post-secondary education and services for Alabama and the region.

The basic mission of IHERS was carried out through studies and reports of value to the state and its educational institutions; cooperative relationships with other institutions and agencies; service projects providing opportunities for pre- and in-service development of faculty members, administrators, trustees, and other groups; and consultative services.

IHERS served as a coordinating unit for a consortium of seven institutions which had program activities in the areas of learning problems, faculty development, curriculum and instructional improvement, joint use of facilities, and regional development planning. In addition, IHERS was the unit of the University responsible for assisting developing colleges through provisions of Title III of the Higher Education Act of 1965.

Throughout the six years that IHERS was operating on campus, it pursued six areas or themes:

* *The Human Resources Development Program* of IHERS included post-secondary education internships for minority persons and women; training two-year college faculty to work with disadvantaged students; helping develop and manage a summer program for high school graduates not bound for college but with college potential; and offering pre- and post-doctoral training opportunities for leaders in post-secondary education.

* An extensive *program of institutional development and cooperative arrangements* between The University of Alabama and other colleges and universities in Alabama as well as in other states which included formal University relations with eighteen other institutions under Title III of the Higher Education Act. It encouraged special bilateral relations with, among others, Stillman College in Tuscaloosa, T.A. Lawson State Community College in Birmingham, and Mary Holms College in West Point, Mississippi.

The program emphasized curriculum reform, improvement of instruction, strengthening of management systems and services to students, and the extension of educational opportunities to non-traditional students.

Through IHERS, the University continued to play a leadership role in the Alabama Consortium for the Development of Higher Education (ACDHE), a cooperative arrangement including colleges, universities, and specialized training institutions in Alabama.

* A number of *studies* were completed by IHERS. These included studies dealing with the future of post-secondary education in Alabama, minority participation in the professions in Alabama, and black graduate students in the state. Other studies included manpower in Alabama, future college enrollments, financial barriers preventing access by Alabama citizens to post-secondary education, and other aspects of poverty in Alabama. A number of other studies were undertaken by IHERS.

* IHERS published the *Handbook of Simulation/Gaming in Social Education*, which received wide acclaim throughout the country and was adopted as a textbook by many universities. Another significant publication was *Blacks in Alabama*, a reference work on age, sex, and residence characteristics of blacks in the state. Other publications included monographs on adult learners in Alabama.

* *Workshops* for citizens on issues and trends in post-secondary education were conducted by the Institute. In 1975–76 alone, conferences on federal affairs, basic skills (reading, writing, listening, speaking), career development, and the metric system served over 300 professional faculty and staff members in colleges and universities located throughout Alabama, the Southeast, and Midwest.

* *Consultation services* were part of the mission of IHERS. By 1975–76, IHERS provided advisory services to a

CCS

TELEVISION WAS USED DURING A MOCK TRIAL AT A CONFERENCE FOR JUDGES
MOUNTED BY THE THE ALABAMA PROGRAM OF CONTINUING LEGAL EDUCATION,
CIRCA 1970.

variety of national and regional agencies, to other colleges and universities in the Southeast, and to a number
of units within the University. Typical agencies assisted
included the American Association of Higher Education, the National Association for Foreign Student
Affairs, and the Alabama Commission on Higher
Education.

Also noted in a 1975–76 progress report on IHERS was the
fact that a sizable increase in the number of research projects
undertaken, publications issued or underway, and conferences
offered was due in part to a generous $118,000 grant from the
Carnegie Corporation of New York. This was the second
Carnegie grant that the Institute had received; the grant enabled it to enlarge its programs and add significantly to its
range of services.

In its six-year life, the Institute of Higher Education and
Research Services accomplished a great deal to promote research in the area of post-secondary education in Alabama and
the Southeastern region. In 1976, IHERS relocated to the
Office for Academic Affairs in the University's central administration.

The Extension Division Renamed
Extended Services, 1970

One change that Dr. Drewry proposed to the University administration as early as 1969 involved image-building to strengthen the powerbase of continuing education. In 1970, the Extension Division was renamed Extended Services. At that time it was composed of a number of units, including a continuing education division. A more unified name and a centralized organizational structure set the tone for Extended Services' mission as Dr. Drewry envisioned it.

As Dr. Drewry noted in his earlier letter to Academic Affairs and in the "Expanding Services . . . " planning document, a major goal of the division staff was to acquire an adequate physical plant for continuing education on the University campus. In 1971, Larry T. McGehee, Roy W. Killingsworth, and Galen Drewry approached President David Mathews about possible sites for construction of the Continuing Education Center. The area that they recommended was not the one ultimately chosen for the Bryant Conference Center and Hotel, opened in the fall of 1987. However, their second choice—"the urban renewal area directly across 10th Street from the Coliseum"—later did become the site for the complex which currently includes the Conference Center and adjacent Sheraton Capstone Inn, the Bryant Museum, and Alumni Hall. They noted that this site would not be available for three to four years or longer "because of uncertainty about financing of urban renewal projects." In fact, the project was off and on for a number of years, but finally was begun in earnest in 1983 when University president Dr. Joab Thomas initiated the project to build the complex.

1970

EXTENSION DIVISION RENAMED EXTENDED SERVICES.

CCS

Ann Jordan Lodge provided a rural retreat for small conferences, meetings, or faculty and staff from 1971–85.

Ann Jordan Lodge—an Off-Campus Retreat

In addition to its Continuing Education Center on campus, Extended Services operated Ann Jordan Lodge in Coosa County 125 miles from Tuscaloosa as an off-campus living/learning center from 1971 until 1985. The lodge was a gift of Mr. Sidney A. Mitchell and his father, the late Sidney Z. Mitchell, to the University and served as a recreational and conference facility for University personnel. Its acreage included the home place of the Jordan family.

The facility was available both for University-sponsored and non-University groups as a conference center, and also as a recreational facility for faculty, staff, and their families. The lodge, motel, and food service accommodated up to sixty people and recreational features such as hiking, fishing in four lakes, and swimming were available. Ann Jordan Lodge offered about 600 acres to visitors for hiking and exploration, with the total parcel of land being about 7,500 acres.

Ann Jordan Lodge served the University well for fourteen years but was closed as a conference and recreation center in 1985. In 1986 management of Ann Jordan Lodge was turned over to the University Office of Land Management.

Highlights of 1971–1972

Reporting to University president Dr. David Mathews in June 1972, Dr. Drewry noted that Extended Services experienced a 21 percent increase over the previous year to a total of 44,116 participants in conferences, seminars, and short courses. Growth in the division could also be seen in new credit course enrollments, which increased 12 percent to a total of 3,893. At this time, Dr. Drewry noted, the division also continued to "conduct continuing education activities throughout the state in cities both large and small."

Dr. Drewry singled out the move to the west tower and most of the first floor of Martha Parham West Hall into a temporary Continuing Education Center as a "major step forward." Now that offices and classes were no longer dispersed about the campus, administration of the unit would be smoother. And more space would increase the possibility of program growth.

MARTHA PARHAM WEST, CIRCA 1970.

Other highlights Dr. Drewry mentioned in the 1972 report to Dr. Mathews included:

* establishment of a Bureau of Performing and Visual Arts to permit quality faculty and student productions to be taken to the communities of the state,
* completion of additional housing units at Ann Jordan Lodge, thereby permitting larger groups to utilize that facility,
* transfer of the Cooperative Education Program organizationally to Extended Services (thus making it a recognized University-wide activity),
* establishment of a Cooperative University Upper Division Program in Gadsden in conjunction with Jacksonville State University,
* initiation of non-credit correspondence courses to complement its Independent Study Department credit offerings,
* recognition of the effectiveness of the Institute of Higher Education by its becoming an assisting agency in eighteen Title III programs, eleven with junior colleges and seven with senior colleges,
* signing of an agreement between The University of Alabama and Brewer State Junior College for the offering of cooperative programs,
* achievement of two firsts by Educational Television: broadcasting of *Androcles and the Lion* on national television and offering of two graduate credit courses in higher education,
* establishment of the Law Enforcement Academy.

Several of the "highlights" in Drewry's 1972 report to Dr. Mathews held long-range significance for continuing education. Among these were the transfer of the Cooperative Education Program, the establishment of the Cooperative University Upper Division (CUUP) program, and the establishment of the Law Enforcement Academy.

Cooperative University Upper Division Program (CUUP)

In 1970, the Cooperative University Upper Division Program (CUUP) in Gadsden was initiated in conjunction with Jacksonville State University and Gadsden State Junior College. This program enabled students who had completed two years at Gadsden State to earn four-year degrees from either Jacksonville State University or The University of Alabama by taking the upper division courses required on the campus of Gadsden State. The program was administered by Dr. James Condra, who had become Gadsden Center director in 1969.

Students wishing to earn a degree from Jacksonville State took "off-campus" courses from that institution which were taught by Jacksonville State at Gadsden State Junior College. The same held true for students wishing to receive a degree from the University. Upper division credit was generally interchangeable, though not completely.

CUUP served as a model of cooperation between two state higher education institutions and served the need of students in the Gadsden area who wished to earn a four-year degree without relocating. A line-item in the state education budget provided for this program until it was deleted in 1986.

1970

COOPERATIVE UNIVERSITY UPPER DIVISION PROGRAM BEGINS IN GADSDEN IN CONJUNCTION WITH JACKSONVILLE STATE UNIVERSITY AND GADSDEN STATE JUNIOR COLLEGE.

James Condra

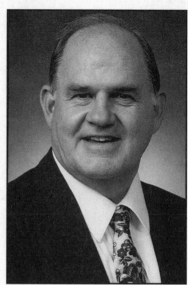

UNIVERSITY RELATIONS

Dr. James Condra was appointed director of the Gadsden Center in 1969. Dr. Condra found a modest credit offering in place, with approximately 50 undergraduates and 85 graduate students being served. At that time, students could take only 12 graduate hours at the Gadsden Center. Undergraduates could work through the sophomore year.

With the guidance of Dr. Condra and his staff, in cooperation with officials on the main campus, the Center evolved from offering the first two years of undergraduate study to offering a full four-year program in selected fields: history, political science, English, and American studies. These programs at Gadsden required no residency at the main campus. In other areas such as commerce and business administration and education, students could take three years of courses at the Gadsden Center and complete the senior year on campus in Tuscaloosa.

The master's degree and course work toward the Ed.S. degree and the doctoral program were also available in education. Graduate courses from the College of Arts and Sciences that supported secondary education, such as English, math and history, were added.

In this way the Gadsden Center met an important need for teachers in the north Alabama area who wanted to complete a master's degree in secondary education and do further course work toward a doctorate in at least three fields.

In 1970–71, the Alabama state legislature passed an appropriation that awarded the University and Jacksonville State University $200,000 each to offer junior and senior year course work at Gadsden State Junior College. The Cooperative University Upper Division Program (CUUP) represented a compromise on the issue of whether or not to make Gadsden State Junior College a four-year institution. CUUP was in place from 1971 to 1986 when the line-item appropriation was dropped. After that time Jacksonville continued to offer courses at Gadsden State but the University did not.

Non-credit offerings at the Gadsden Center during this time included a number of offerings in business and industry through Title I administered by Continuing Education Services for Small Businesses and Industries. This program presented seminars and in-house programs in the Gadsden area and around the state.

In addition to offering a much-needed slate of credit courses and degree programs, the Gadsden Center sponsored non-credit activities for teachers. A popular Dinner Seminar program was initiated which included a meal and an evening seminar on timely topics such as school law or instructional techniques. Many teachers in the Gadsden area availed themselves of these professional development opportunities which were taught both by University faculty and by outside practitioners.

During 1983–86, Dr. Condra and the Gadsden Center staff participated in developing two consortia for professional development for educators. One was the Northeast Consortium for Professional Development which included five school systems representing nearly 2,800 teachers. The other was the Gadsden Consortium for Professional Development which consisted of seven school systems with about 1,200 teachers.

These consortia offered a large menu of workshops and served 2,000–3,000 participants per year. The workshops could be taken as non-credit professional development work or students could arrange to receive credit by taking blocks of workshops and paying additional tuition.

The Gadsden Center-initiated consortia were the antecedents of the Alabama Regional In-Service Education Centers, first funded in 1985 by the state of Alabama. Eleven centers were funded to serve teachers throughout Alabama, with the program continuing to the present day. In Gadsden, the In-Service Education Center at Jacksonville and Alabama A & M universities replaced the consortia to serve teachers in that area.

The University of Alabama began working cooperatively out of the main campus with Livingston University to serve 12 school systems from Tuscaloosa to Choctaw counties. Jill Shearin, formerly with the Gadsden Center, headed the UA/Livingston University In-Service Education Center from 1986 to the present.

The Gadsden Center also provided a testing service for the Gadsden-Etowah County area, offering the General Education Development Test, the Miller Analogies Test, the Scholastic Aptitude Test, the American College Test, the Graduate Record Examination, and others.

Dr. Condra also participated in the placement of student teachers who wished to complete their student teaching experience in the Gadsden area.

In July of 1985, Dr. Condra returned to the main campus to become assistant dean for Administration and Finance in the College of Education.

Since 1976, the Gadsden Center has played an important role as the only remaining University of Alabama extension center. By continuing to explore people's needs and marshalling the resources of the University to meet those needs, the Center has been successful in extending the resources of the University in a way that positively impacts individuals, as well as the educational system of the state.

Law Enforcement Academy Established

On September 1, 1972, the Law Enforcement Academy was established within Extended Services in response to a state mandate for training for all new law enforcement officers. The University Academy was one of three in the state, the other two being housed at Jacksonville State University and the University of South Alabama.

The Academy's mission was to provide entry-level training to law enforcement professionals and reserve officers. Although a task force had been set up and had estimated that it would take one year before the Academy could become operational, just two weeks later on September 15, 1972, the first session of Basic Training for law enforcement officers began.

CCS

THE LAW ENFORCEMENT ACADEMY GRADUATED ITS FIRST SESSION IN 1972, UNDER THE DIRECTION OF CAPT. RUSSELL L. SUMMERLIN (FAR RIGHT, FIRST ROW).

The curriculum at this time consisted of 240 hours of instruction for which a participant received nine semester credit hours from the University. In 1981, this was increased to 280 hours, with 12 semester credit hours being awarded for successful completion of the course.

Capt. Russell Summerlin was appointed director of the Academy, a position in which he served until 1990.

The first advanced training program was also held in September 1972 in conjunction with the Department of Psychology. Nationally recognized instructors were brought in for this seminar, including the director of the Federal Bureau of Investigation. The two 14-week advanced training sessions, called the "Law Enforcement Institute," were awarded 21 semester credit hours.

In 1978, a Correction Academy began and two sessions were run for the Alabama Department of Corrections at which time the Department established its own academy in Selma.

In 1991, the Law Enforcement Academy graduated its 100th session of Basic Training.

"I AM VERY PROUD OF THE FACT THAT THE ACADEMY SET THE PACE FOR LAW ENFORCEMENT TRAINING IN ALABAMA AND WAS SELECTED AS THE STATE'S MODEL AGENCY FOR NON-DISCRIMINATORY TRAINING BY THE U. S. DEPARTMENT OF JUSTICE."

UNIVERSITY RELATIONS

CAPT. RUSSELL L. SUMMERLIN

Col. Joe M. Gelwix

"IT IS THE LITTLE THINGS THAT MAKE A PROGRAM A SUCCESS AND MAKE CONFEREES FEEL IMPORTANT. FOR A PROGRAM TO SUCCEED, YOU HAVE TO BE AVAILABLE AND RESPONSIBLE TO PEOPLE'S NEEDS. IN THE DIVISION WE WERE AVAILABLE TO HELP ANYONE, AND I AM PROUD TO HAVE BEEN A PART OF THE ORGANIZATION."

Col. Joe M. Gelwix joined the Extension Division in fall 1969 as coordinator of Continuing Education for Government Employees, administering training programs through the federally funded Title I program. Among the groups he served were city clerks, state employees, revenue officers, city administrators and engineers, juvenile probation officers, probate judges, and county administrators.

Col. Gelwix also coordinated programs for librarians and teachers, including educators in Gadsden and Dothan. Other programs that he coordinated included the Natural Gas Distribution workshops and programs for personnel in labor/management and parks and recreation.

Col. Gelwix worked extensively with the Alabama League of Municipalities which was instrumental in the growth of many municipal programs. Col. Gelwix called the League "the springboard of our success for launching new programs."

Other activities with which Col. Gelwix were associated included assisting in setting up the Law Enforcement Academy and coordinating the original orientation program for current and newly-elected state legislators. In 1973, Dr. Drewry asked Col. Gelwix to serve as acting director of Continuing Education during the search for a director.

Col. Gelwix retired in 1979.

The Continuing Education Unit (CEU) Is Adopted by the Southern Association of Colleges and Schools

One of the significant highlights of the 1971–72 year was the adoption of a totally revised Standard IX by the Southern Association of Colleges and Schools. Dr. Drewry believed that this would have "far-reaching effects in the future." He noted that the new standard increased greatly the flexibility for conducting special activities and provided for the continuing education unit (CEU) as a measure of continuing education work. "The CEU will provide a framework on which extended certificate and external degree programs will be built," Dr. Drewry predicted.

Policies and Procedures Are Clarified

The early 1970s were a time of organization and clarification, as well as planning. As Dr. Drewry led the division in a period of growth, he outlined policy guidelines for conferences, short courses, and seminar groups at the continuing education center. He stressed that "the primary focus of the proposed activity (i.e., conference, short course, or seminar) should be educational in nature" and "that the activity have the sanction of some college, school, department, or other unit or agency of The University of Alabama." These guidelines were designed to further strengthen the position of continuing education on campus and increase its academic credibility.

While Dr. Drewry's goals were becoming realities, changes did not come as quickly or as easily as he hoped.

Restructuring and Staffing in Continuing Education

In 1973, the Division of Continuing Education within Extended Services was assessed with an eye to updating it and

---

1970

Ann Jordan Lodge in Coosa County assigned to Extended Services as a conference and retreat facility.

---

restructuring some of its arrangements and responsibilities. Also at this time, the position of director of Continuing Education was proposed. This updating served to clarify that area, to which the following offices now reported: instructional services, conferences and short courses, independent study, special adult studies, and continuing education center management services.

For a number of months Dr. Drewry and his staff screened applications for director of Continuing Education. In August, Dr. Drewry appointed Col. Joe M. Gelwix acting director. Col. Gelwix served until Dr. William Bryan was named director of Continuing Education in 1975.

Dr. Drewry Keeps UA Administration Informed about Continuing Education Trends and Concerns

Perhaps one of Dr. Drewry's greatest contributions to the development of continuing education as an educational delivery system at The University of Alabama was his ability to articulate trends. In a memo to Dr. Howard Gundy, academic vice-president, in August 1973, Dr. Drewry laid out what he saw as the future of Extended Services. He noted that "there is widespread agreement across the whole county that continuing education is the cutting edge, the growth factor in higher education for at least the near future. Many institutions and individuals who have had only a disdainful glance for continuing education earlier are making their play." Drewry pointed out that private entities were getting into the business of continuing education and not always delivering a quality product.

He delineated for Dr. Gundy some of his concerns about the need for systematic growth in continuing education at the

1970-74

DEVELOPMENT OF OFF-CAMPUS PROGRAMS EXPANDED.

University. Dr. Drewry had from the beginning of his deanship put the vital concerns of continuing education before the University administration. Of particular concern to Dr. Drewry were the limitations on Extended Services' ability to offer credit, the lack of approval to provide adult study programs having degree objectives, and the serious limitations of Martha Parham West as a continuing education center.

Extended Services Staff Proposes Future Programs

At the same time, Dr. Drewry's leadership ability and nurturance in the evolution of continuing education at The University of Alabama were reflected in his efforts to lead his staff to use the best of their talents and ideas during this period of restructuring, global planning, and growth.

In 1973, Dr. Drewry appointed a contingent of task forces to study various aspects of future development. These included task forces to study: 1) the best use of the Continuing Education Center, 2) program development, 3) cooperative efforts with junior colleges in continuing education, and 4) quarterly staff meetings and seminars.

In late 1973 and early 1974, Dr. Drewry and the staff of Extended Services participated in planning sessions that would help shape continuing education at the University for years to come. Excerpts from Dr. Drewry's letter of January 7, 1974, to Dr. Gundy reflect Dr. Drewry's enthusiasm for the possibilities his staff had touched upon in an intensive "working party" in which they spent two full days studying, consolidating, revising, and refining 49 proposals for new programs submitted by 25 different staff members:

"During recent weeks the staff of Extended Services has been engaged in one of the most exciting, and, I feel, most

1971

OFFICE OF EXTENDED INSTRUCTIONAL PROGRAMS CREATED.

productive activities in recent years," Dr. Drewry wrote. "In November, the staff was invited to submit proposals for major new programs or major expansion of present programs.... A few of these were 'single-shot' proposals for a particular conference or short course. Interestingly, several duplicates came from staff members who were unaware others were submitting a similar proposal."

Dr. Drewry went on to explain that at the two-day retreat, each member had the opportunity to consider each of the 49 proposals. Out of this session came eight proposed programs which the party agreed should have high priority as additional funds became available from regular sources for augmenting the continuing education program of The University of Alabama. Dr. Drewry believed deeply in the value of personal development within a professional setting, and he knew the "working party" exercise was one of growth for the staff: "If no other tangible results ever materialize from this exercise, I believe it was an invaluable experience for us to spend this time thinking about and discussing program development for Extended Services." Copies of the proposals were forwarded with the letter to Dr. Gundy.

Programs proposed were: Continuing Education Field Services, Advanced Law Enforcement Institute, Expanded Continuing Education Services for Business and Industry, Institute for Community Development and Continuing Education Services, Expanded Cooperative Education Program, Metric Education Center, Instructional Support Services, and Continuing Education Information.

1971-72

CONTINUING EDUCATION UNIT (CEU) ADOPTED AS A MEASURE OF CONTINUING EDUCATION WORK BY THE SOUTHERN ASSOCIATION OF COLLEGES AND SCHOOLS (AS PART OF THE REVISED STANDARD IX).

Dr. Drewry Reports to Vice-President Sutton on
Significant Events of 1969–1974

In 1974, Dr. Drewry reported to Dr. Joseph T. Sutton, then vice-president for Institutional Research, on "significant events of the last five years." They included operations of the University in the Gadsden area, the establishment and operation of the Institute of Higher Education Research and Services, establishment of the Law Enforcement Academy, and the adoption of the CEU as a measure of participation in continuing education.

Also, by 1974 it was becoming apparent that a facility such as the Continuing Education Center in Martha Parham West, offering clean, attractive, and comfortable space for educational programs with convenient dining and lodging facilities would attract new programs. Dr. Drewry noted in his report to Dr. Sutton that the Law Enforcement Academy, counseling workshops, and banker's and school administrator's conferences were examples of programs that were awarded to The University of Alabama primarily because a continuing education facility was available. And the future would prove that as Extended Services' programs continued to grow, and as the adult learner population increased, there would be an increasingly strong argument for construction of a dedicated, state-of-the-art continuing education facility.

Special Adult Studies

The Special Adult Studies office was created in 1971 as a response to the educational needs—both credit and non-credit—of adults in the Tuscaloosa area. Non-credit leisure

---

1972

COOPERATIVE EDUCATION REASSIGNED TO EXTENDED SERVICES FROM COLLEGE OF ENGINEERING, THUS MAKING THE CO-OP PROGRAM AVAILABLE TO ALL UNIVERSITY STUDENTS.

---

learning and self-help courses in a variety of areas were offered. Typical classes included gourmet cooking, basic landscaping, and parliamentary procedure.

In addition to these non-credit courses, Special Adult Studies also administered PACE, the Program for Adults Continuing Their Education, on a part-time basis. It provided assistance to adults interested in part-time credit study, including admission options, an orientation program, and general information about University services. PACE served as a point of entry for the adult student who did not plan to be enrolled full-time at the University.

Independent Study

A significant event for the Independent Study Division in 1974–75 was updating high school correspondence courses. Through a cooperative arrangement between The University of Alabama and the Alabama Education Association, eighteen teachers spent a week in the summer of 1974 revamping courses for grades 9 through 12. The courses were patterned as closely as possible on instruction provided in the high school classrooms throughout the state, using textbooks approved by the state textbook committee. Several new courses were added, among them Alabama History, Sociology, Unified Geometry, and Consumer Mathematics. The courses were refined and edited in the fall and made available in January 1975.

MARY COE

Mary Coe's 34-year career in continuing education began in 1943 when she was hired as secretary to Dr. R. E. Tidwell. Later she became assistant to Dr. John Morton.

Miss Coe counts among the highlights during her tenure in

the dean's office watching the establishment and growth of Extension Centers in Birmingham, Montgomery, Mobile, and later in Huntsville, Gadsden, Dothan, and Selma. She also enjoyed working with faculty members from across the Tuscaloosa campus, assisting with the administration of their courses.

As assistant to the dean from the mid-1950s to 1970, she was assigned the major responsibility of managing budgets for the various Centers across the state.

In 1970, Dr. Drewry asked Miss Coe to assume the role of director of Independent Study upon Clarice Parker's retirement. Some of the changes Miss Coe instituted included increasing independent study engineering courses, adding a physics course, and expanding offerings in Arts and Sciences, Commerce and Business Administration, and Education.

Improvements were also made in the high school independent study program already in place, including modeling new courses on those from the University of Nebraska and employing Tuscaloosa area high school teachers as well as those teaching on college level to teach in the program.

Miss Coe retired in July 1977 and now lives in St. Petersburg, Florida.

The Development of Off-Campus Credit Activities, 1970–1974

On September 1, 1970, the University established the Office of Off-Campus Graduate Courses. This office was given the primary responsibility of extending the University's credit course offerings to citizens throughout the state. The estab-

---

1972

FIRST SESSION OF BASIC TRAINING HELD IN THE NEWLY ESTABLISHED LAW ENFORCEMENT ACADEMY.

the challenge of
Tomorrow

**BEGINS
TODAY . . . at the
UNIVERSITY
OF
ALABAMA
GADSDEN CENTER**
121 NORTH FIRST STREET

Students may now complete all requirements for the Masters Degree in selected areas of study at the University of Alabama Gadsden Center.

CCS

lishment of this office signified the University's reaffirmation of providing off-campus credit work. At the request of President David Mathews, Dr. L. Tennent Lee took responsibility for seeing that the program was properly launched.

The Office's role was strengthened considerably by linking it to all University academic units. Guidelines for establishing off-campus graduate courses, in accordance with Standard IX of the Southern Association of Colleges and Schools, were communicated to University faculty.

Although the Office worked initially with the College of Education, off-campus credit courses from other academic divisions could now be delivered to off-campus sites by mutual agreement. The major thrust of the Office focused upon the delivery of off-campus graduate credit course work from the University's professional schools.

During the 1974–75 academic year, the Office became known as the Office of Extended Instructional Programs and Services. At that time the staff consisted of a director, one secretary, and one registrar. In addition to off-campus programs the Office was given the responsibility of coordinating the financial procedures associated with the External Degree Program. Later External Degree was moved to New College.

Groundwork was laid during Dr. Drewry's tenure for the growth of off-campus programs, an extremely valuable program with Extension Services which continues to thrive in the College of Continuing Studies in the 1990s by meeting the needs of adults desiring undergraduate and graduate degree credit.

Dr. L. Tennent Lee

"I FEEL MY GREATEST CONTRIBUTION TO CONTINUING EDUCATION WAS ESTABLISHMENT OF THE OFFICE OF OFF-CAMPUS GRADUATE COURSES. WE BEGAN TO SERVE WORKING PEOPLE IN THE FIELDS OF EDUCATION, HOME ECONOMICS, AND ENGINEERING WHO WERE TRYING TO PURSUE GRADUATE DEGREES WHILE THEY EARNED A LIVING AND SUPPORTED FAMILIES. WE TRULY EXTENDED THE UNIVERSITY'S SERVICES TO THE PEOPLE OF THE STATE.

I AM ALSO PROUD OF OUR ATTEMPTS AT COOPERATION WITH OTHER INSTITUTIONS OF HIGHER EDUCATION IN ALABAMA, SUCH AS THE UNIVERSITY OF MONTEVALLO, WHICH HAD SIMILAR GOALS IN MIND."

UNIVERSITY RELATIONS

Dr. L. Tennent Lee's work in the field of higher education began in the 1940s when Dr. Robert Tidwell was building the Extension program at the University. Although Dr. Lee did not formally work with continuing education until shortly before his retirement, the experience and dedication that he brought to the division enabled him to have a major impact in just three years, from 1970–73.

Prior to working with continuing education, Dr. Lee had served as chairman of the Department of Secondary Education at the University and subsequently was offered the job of director of Summer School and assistant graduate dean, a position he held from 1960–70.

In 1970, he was approached by President Mathews to work in continuing education as administrative coordinator of Services to the Professions. He would also serve as associate dean for Continuing Education in the College of Education.

Dr. Lee was charged with developing a more positive relationship between the University and the elementary and secondary school systems of the state. For the first year he worked to establish a rapport between the two constituencies, hosting dinners for principals and school superintendents statewide.

Also during the first year he centralized the administration of off-campus graduate courses. Until this time, the various colleges on campus had offered their own courses and administered them individually. Dr. Lee set up campuswide guiding principles, sanctioned by the President's office, stating who could register students for off-campus graduate courses, as well as making other administrative procedures clear.

During the second year, the Office of Campus Graduate Courses was opened in the Division of Continuing Education. A number of graduate courses in education, home economics, and engineering were offered at locations around the state. Dr. Lee supervised the administration of these courses, many of which required that the professor register students and collect registration fees on-site. By the third year of the program, there were 1,700 enrollments in graduate courses taught off-campus. Thus a major need was addressed—providing graduate course work to working professionals who could not leave jobs to attend classes on campus.

At this time, federal education grants were readily available for improving education. Dr. Lee worked with various school systems that had received federal monies to set up courses. In

Decatur, Dr. Lee worked with the City School System on a proposed curriculum revision. Dovetailing with this was Dr. Lee's belief that turf wars among the various colleges and universities in the state regarding graduate education off-campus should be minimized. Dr. Lee believed cooperative efforts were the way to such avoid such conflicts. For the Decatur Schools project, he employed a University of Alabama professor and a University of Montevallo professor to conduct the courses. Students in Decatur could take off-campus courses for credit from either University. Had he not retired, Dr. Lee had planned to set up similar programs in other cities.

In 1974, the division established the Office of Extended Programs and Services, thus continuing The University of Alabama's commitment to serving the needs of professionals seeking graduate degrees.

Dr. Robert Leigh

"WE WERE ABLE TO BE FLEXIBLE AT A TIME WHEN THERE WAS A GREAT DEAL OF NEED TO OFFER INSTRUCTION IN NON-TRADITIONAL FORMATS. THE UNIVERSITY WAS WILLING TO SERVE PEOPLE AND THEY LOOKED TO US TO PROVIDE THAT SERVICE. THIS ENABLED US TO BE LEADERS AT A TIME WHEN CONTINUING EDUCATION WAS REALLY COMING INTO ITS OWN. WITH THE LEADERSHIP OF PEOPLE LIKE DR. L. TENNENT LEE AND DR. GALEN DREWRY WE PROVIDED WHAT WAS NEEDED, WHEN IT WAS NEEDED. AND WE'VE BEEN BUILDING ON THAT TRUST IN OUR SERVICE EVER SINCE."

Dr. Robert Leigh, associate professor in the College of Education, began working with Extension Services in 1969–70 in conjunction with Dr. L. Tennent Lee at the time that off-campus programs were being developed. Dr. Leigh and Dr. L. Tennent Lee, who was associate dean of Education and ad-

UNIVERSITY RELATIONS

IN 1992, DR. ROBERT LEIGH RECEIVED THE COLLEGE OF CONTINUING STUDIES'
EIGHTH ANNUAL AWARD FOR TEACHING EXCELLENCE. REGGIE SMITH, ASSOCIATE
DEAN OF THE COLLEGE, AND UNIVERSITY PRESIDENT DR. ROGER SAYERS PARTICI-
PATED IN THE CEREMONY.

ministrative coordinator of Services to the Professions,
teamed up to develop courses that would be delivered at
various places across the state. Teachers and supervisors in
such towns as Greenville, Fayette, and Albertville took advantage of these off-campus education courses.

During the early 1970s, Dr. Leigh helped offer a course that
was delivered in part using Educational Television (ETV).
Approximately 125 teachers signed up for the course, with
about 75 receiving credit. ETV broadcasts of instruction were
made twice a week and then students met with the professors
in person at various sites around the state to discuss how to
implement some of the things at their local unit level that they
had learned.

Dr. Leigh also taught early childhood and reading courses
on a regular basis at the Gadsden Center for a number of years,
counseling many teachers in that area who were working
toward graduate degrees.

One program that Dr. Leigh was instrumental in starting continued in 1992. GIFT (Good Ideas For Teaching), brings teachers to campus from across the state to develop instructional modules which are then published and delivered to the teachers at the local level. Specially selected teachers and supervisors may receive undergraduate or graduate credit for GIFT work. Published GIFT instruction books have been used by educators nationally and internationally.

Dr. Leigh and others in Extended Services and the College of Education worked together to set up The University of Alabama Instructional Assistance Center which mounted programs to assist schools as they integrated teaching faculties in the late 1960s and early 1970s. School superintendents looked to the University for assistance in complying with federal guidelines, and Dr. Leigh was able to help set up workshops in this area for which supervisors and teachers could receive credit.

Although he officially retired from the University in 1990 as Professor Emeritus of Curriculum and Instruction, Dr. Leigh continues to work enthusiastically toward providing academic opportunities for teachers of adult education. He serves as a mentor for teachers, providing guidance and moral support, and continues to be an active advocate for adult education throughout the state, working closely with the Alabama State Department of Education in developing educational programs.

In 1992, Dr. Leigh received the eighth Award for Teaching Excellence, an annual award given by the College of Continuing Studies.

1972

CONTINUING EDUCATION CENTER IN MARTHA PARHAM WEST OPENS; ATTENDANCE IN CONFERENCES, SHORT COURSES, AND SEMINARS CONTINUES TO INCREASE.

UNIVERSITY RELATIONS

THE HEAD START SUPPLEMENTARY TRAINING PROGRAM IN ALABAMA PROVIDED
TEACHERS OF PRESCHOOL CHILDREN BASIC TEACHING SKILLS.

Head Start, a National Model for Teacher Training

In 1970, the Division of Continuing Education became
responsible for operation of the Head Start Supplementary
Training (HSST) program in Alabama. At that time, no training for college credit was being conducted for Head Start
personnel in the area. In 1971, 25 employees from Head Start
centers in Greene, Pickens, and Sumter counties began a series
of cluster classes on the University campus. The typical en-

1973

DR. WILLIAM B. BRYAN ASSUMES NEW DUTIES AND RESPONSIBILITIES AS DIRECTOR,
EXTENDED INSTRUCTIONAL PROGRAMS AND SERVICES.

---

rollee was a black woman over 35 years of age, with no previous college experience. Through the offerings provided, most of the trainees earned 18–21 semester credit hours, all in courses related to their work with children under six.

According to the November 1974 report on Head Start accompanying Dr. Drewry's report to Dr. Sutton, success stories in Head Start training were numerous. Miss Bethel Fite, director of Library and Program Services who also administered HSST wrote, "One student with previous college work completed the requirements for her degree and had full-time employment as a child welfare worker in the state merit system. Another, on the basis of her academic record in the program and her work record, was awarded a full scholarship in a four-year college. A number of the students were promoted because of the new competencies they had acquired."

In 1974, HSST was replaced with the Child Development Associate competency-based program, which allowed for the addition of directed individual study in the field to the cluster classes already in place.

Students could complete credit courses applicable toward a degree in child development while at the same time preparing for assessment for a national, professional credential, the CDA credential.

* * *

In February 1975, Dr. Howard Gundy, academic vice-president, announced to the staff of Extended Services that Dr. Drewry would be resigning as associate academic vice president and dean of Extended Services effective March 1. Dr. Gundy named Dr. Bryan, then director of Continuing Education, to coordinate the total efforts of Continuing Education and Extended Services on an acting basis. All extension and continuing education activities became grouped under the

1973

CONTINUING LEGAL EDUCATION BECOMES A PART OF THE LAW SCHOOL.

heading, Division of Continuing Education. Dr. Bryan was named dean of the Division of Continuing Education in 1977.

Dr. Drewry saw the shape of things to come for continuing education from a global perspective. He understood that the old idea of extension, meaning to export instruction from the central campus out to the state, must give way to a broader, more complex notion of continuing education which involved both taking instruction to the people and bringing the people to the central campus either literally or via telecommunications. Dr. Drewery articulated to University administrators the national trend of a widening circle of people who could potentially be touched by continuing education. Though he spent a shorter time at the helm than any of his predecessors, Dr. Drewry's vision for a blueprint of continuing education's future—from the need for expanded programming to the necessity of a dedicated meeting facility—and his continual articulation of that vision for the administration helped move the University toward better serving the needs of adult learners in future years.

1974

THE CHILD DEVELOPMENT ASSOCIATE (CDA) TRAINING PROGRAM REPLACES HEADSTART, ALLOWING STUDENTS TO COMPLETE CREDIT COURSES APPLICABLE TO A DEGREE WHILE PREPARING FOR THE CDA CREDENTIAL.

1974-75

HIGH SCHOOL INDEPENDENT STUDY COURSES UPDATED.

CHAPTER 6

MAINTAINING QUALITY PROGRAMS

Era of Dr. William B. Bryan, 1975–1983

DR. WILLIAM B. BRYAN

UNIVERSITY RELATIONS

For the two years following Dr. Galen Drewry's resignation as associate academic vice-president and dean of Extended Services in March 1975, the Division of Extended Services was in a period of transition. Dr. William Bryan was named acting director of the Division during this time. His position was made permanent as dean of the Division of Continuing Education in 1977. At the same time Dr. Bryan was named dean, various parts of Extended Services were reorganized under the title Division of Continuing Education.

On-going, high-quality programs such as the Law Enforcement Academy, Independent Study, Library Services, Off-Campus Programs, and numerous conferences and workshops continued to function.

Dr. Bryan, Dr. Lanny Gamble, and various other staff members conceived of ways to serve the educational needs of adult learners in the state of Alabama by reorganizing, refining, or proposing new, nontraditional programs.

It is important to note that the impetus toward revamping programs and bringing new ones to life that could serve the changing population of potential students of The University of Alabama—for both credit and non-credit courses—was a natural progression from Dr. Drewry's period of leadership. Though many of the proposals did not evolve into actual programs, the Division of Continuing Education's impulse toward alternative delivery of programs tailored to the needs of working adults was on target for the times. Continuing education, especially in the credit area, would continue to evolve as the vehicle by which many would travel on the road to professional or career development.

The Division Seeks Continued Growth, 1975–1976

In a 1975-76 statement of objectives for the Division, Dr. Bryan noted that the program had shown significant growth in 1974-75. He named the Metric Institute, Gadsden Center, Law Enforcement Academy, Conference Activities, and Independent Study as areas that experienced a successful year. In addition, he named four areas of accomplishment which seemed "to have particular implications for the coming year." These were the establishment of Regional Offices in Mobile

---

1975

DR. WILLIAM B. BRYAN NAMED ACTING DIRECTOR OF CONTINUING EDUCATION, ASSUMES RESPONSIBILITIES FOR ALL AREAS THAT FORMERLY REPORTED TO THE DEAN (EXCEPT GADSDEN CENTER).

---

and Dothan (in addition to Gadsden and Montgomery); increased activities of the Office of Extended Instructional Programs and Services; increased utilization of the Continuing Education Center, which had shown a dramatic income increase over the previous year and boasted some 4,000 more conference participants than the year before; and, strengthening of programs for adults continuing their education, with assistance from the Office of Student Services.

Two new efforts for 1975-76 that Dr. Bryan singled out were establishment of a Weekend College at the University and broadening of non-credit programs in conjunction with the Office of Special Adult Studies and University Recreation.

Serving the Adult Learner

In 1978, Dr. Bryan reiterated Dr. Drewry's vision of serving the adult learner: "The Division of Continuing Education encompasses a broad and diverse range of services which continuously changes with the needs of the people of our state. These needs are identified by active, involved faculty and by our own continuing education specialists. These needs also are identified through the actual requests for educational services that are received from individuals and groups throughout Alabama. For these people, the University's response is the key to organization or fiscal success, to professional growth, or to developing a full and rich personal life." Bryan noted that the Division of Continuing Education currently was involved in an evaluation of its administrative structure and all of its programs in an attempt to develop priorities for meeting the educational needs of adults in a more effective manner. He wrote that he hoped this study would result in more responsive programming in the immediate future.

1976

IHERS RELOCATED TO OFFICE OF ACADEMIC AFFAIRS.

Weekend College Begins, 1976

One of the proposed programs which was positively received and came to fruition was Weekend College. During the 1975-76 academic year, the Weekend College program was conceived as an alternative method of delivery of educational opportunities that would better meet the needs of people who could not participate in daytime or evening classes.

In the proposal for Weekend College, evidence from the American Council on Education (ACE) was offered showing that since 1969 more students had participated in post-secondary education on a part-time basis than on a full-time basis. Furthermore, the number of part-time students was apparently increasing more than twice as fast as that of full-time students, according to the ACE.

Dr. Bryan and his staff conceived of Weekend College as a means of serving this new—and rapidly growing—educational market. In the Weekend College proposal, the 1972 proceedings of the Association of University Evening Colleges were also quoted as testament to the Weekend College phenomenon: "The Weekend College may additionally serve as the mechanism for encompassing a new educational market composed of blue and white collar working forces, housewives, members of the armed forces, and those whose job requirements specify shifting every couple of weeks. It may provide the vehicle by which those who have never attended college in the past, or those who attended but left for a variety of reasons and have joined the work force, may return to a collegiate environment."

Weekend College began operation in the 1976 fall semester and during its first year enrolled over 400 students. The Weekend College format provided for classes to meet on Friday nights and most of the day Saturday for four weekends in a

---

1976

WEEKEND COLLEGE MAKES ALTERNATIVE CREDIT COURSE FORMATS AVAILABLE.

---

row during the semester. Contact hours, course requirements, testing, etc., were the same as for those courses offered in the traditional format. Through cooperative relationships with academic divisions, Weekend College offered all course work necessary for master's degrees in several curricula areas. From the outset it was understood that the administration of Weekend College would require the extensive involvement of personnel in other divisions of the University. Once underway, Weekend College proved successful. By the 1979-80 academic year, 1,214 students had participated in Weekend College, and it continued to be a viable program well into the 1990s.

Summer Inter-Semester

A program that might be seen as a sister program to Weekend College was the proposed Summer Inter-Semester. Proposed by the Office of Extended Instructional Programs within the Division of Continuing Education, this program would have consisted of a series of regular academic courses offered in alternative time formats during the summer months. The proposed semester would be offered concurrently with Interim and Summer Sessions and would provide adult, part-time, and full-time students expanded opportunities to enroll in academic programs.

In no way intended to compete with existing schedules, Summer Inter-Semester was presented as a complementary scheduling concept designed to encourage and broaden the scope of existing University course offerings while at the same time increasing student enrollment and use of resources during summer months. One stated objective in the program proposal was "to provide divisional leadership at the University in addressing solutions to problems indicated by current trends in higher education, such as the anticipated decline in

1977

DR. WILLIAM BRYAN NAMED DEAN OF DIVISION OF CONTINUING EDUCATION.

THE 1980s SAW MORE AND MORE ADULT STUDENTS RETURNING TO THE CLASSROOM
FOR ADVANCED DEGREES.

student enrollment, under-utilization of University resources, and special needs of adult learners." The proposal stressed flexibility in programming, again aiming at the part-time or working adult student.

Each course was to be offered in timeframes of two weeks minimum to four weeks maximum. The key to the success of the Summer Inter-Semester, the proposers wrote, would be the scheduling of intensive learning experiences, lasting several hours per session, which would meet both content and contact hour requirements for regular academic courses. Ideally, the Interim, Summer, and Summer Inter-Session, would be complementary delivery mechanisms for academic programs and provide a comprehensive offering of classes to all students. Apparently, however, the time was not right for Summer Inter-Session, and the program did not come to life.

1977

THE OSHA CONSULTANT TRAINING PROGRAM BEGINS WITHIN CONTINUING ENGINEERING EDUCATION.

Other Special Projects in Planning Stages Are
Reported to President Mathews, 1977

In mid-1977, Dr. Bryan brought to the attention of President Mathews some special projects that were to be implemented in 1977–78. Some would require additional staffing and funding and some, he felt, could be accomplished through the transfer of existing staff and funds from other areas of the University.

At the top of the list was the need for a new Continuing Education Center. "This is essential," Dr. Bryant wrote, "if we are to meet the challenges inherent in an effective outreach program of a major state university." Although Dr. Bryan was once again articulating a need for this facility, it would be five more years before the announcement of the University's commitment to build a conference center, alumni hall, and the Bryant Museum.

Other proposals in the memo included moving Interim Term and certain intern programs across campus into the Division of Continuing Education; expanding and sufficiently funding the Center for the Family; and integrating instructional technology such as videotapes, telephone, cable television, audiotapes, and correspondence as a means toward extending educational services and programs. In this latter proposal, Independent Study courses would be repackaged using various technological enhancements.

Alumni College and the Capstone Elderhostel were also proposed as ways of bringing alumni or older students back to campus. The Center for the Study of Aging would work together with the Division on coordination of Elderhostel.

Finally, through joint funding with the College of Commerce and Business Administration, training programs were pro-

---

1977–78

THREE NEW ASSISTANT DEANS ARE APPOINTED AND REPORTING CHANNELS REORGANIZED.

posed to be developed for the private sector. Topics included "Effective World Business Communications," "How to Use Statistical Concepts in Business," "Financial Management for Non-Financial Managers," "Personal Asset Management," and "Management for Employee Benefits." It was hoped that a director of Training Programs could be employed within the Division to facilitate this program. Many of these proposals were included in the five-year plan that went forward to central administration in spring 1978.

Also in the summer of 1977, Dr. Bryan prepared a written statement regarding the mission and long-range plans for Continuing Education. This document helped Division staff prepare the five-year plan shortly thereafter. The mission of the Division of Continuing Education remained consistent with that of the founders of the extension movement, with an ever-increasing emphasis on extending the resources of the institution.

THE MISSION OF THE DIVISION OF CONTINUING EDUCATION IS TO CREATE EFFECTIVE WAYS FOR AS MANY INDIVIDUALS AS POSSIBLE TO CONTINUE THE ACQUISITION OF INFORMATION RELEVANT TO PROFESSIONAL, SOCIAL, AND CULTURAL DEVELOPMENT THROUGHOUT THEIR LIVES. MOREOVER, A FURTHER INTENT OF PROGRAMS IN THE DIVISION IS TO MAKE THE UNIQUE RESOURCES AND CAPABILITIES OF THE UNIVERSITY AVAILABLE TO INCREASINGLY DIVERSE GROUPS WITHIN OUR SOCIETY.
—FROM "DIVISION OF CONTINUING EDUCATION LONG RANGE PLANS"

Reorganization in Effect, 1978

In 1977–78, the Division's organizational structure was modified. Three assistant dean positions were created and reporting channels adjusted accordingly. Dr. James Condra became assistant dean for the Gadsden Programs, Dr. Lanny Gamble assumed the title of assistant dean for Instructional Programs, and Dr. Coy Hollis became assistant dean for Administration.

Reporting to the dean in this new structure were the three assistant deans, the directors of the Regional Offices, the director of the Law Enforcement Academy, and the director of Marketing and Information.

As the title implied, Dr. Condra handled all activities at the Gadsden Center. Dr. Gamble administered programs offered off-campus, Weekend College, correspondence courses, and off-campus master's degree programs. Also at this time, a director of Independent Study was created, broadening the scope of correspondence study.

Dr. Hollis was responsible for the non-credit programs which included Conference Activities, Special Adult Studies, Metric Institute, Government Employee Training, and the directors and coordinators who provided liaison with the academic divisions.

This structure remained in place for approximately the next five years.

First Continuing Education Minor
for Ph.D. Candidates in Education Instituted, 1978

In the spring 1978 semester, the program for a continuing education minor as part of the Ph.D. program in the College of Continuing Education was finalized. The first student was Ms. Ernestine Davis. Ms. Davis began an internship with the Division of Continuing Education that semester, working ten hours per week. Ms. Davis had an office in Martha Parham West and met with the continuing education staff to discuss the role and function of the various offices.

1978

CONTINUING EDUCATION MINOR AVAILABLE FOR PH.D. CANDIDATES IN COLLEGE OF EDUCATION.

Five-year Plan Projects Credit Enrollment Will Increase

In 1978, a five-year planning document addressed the projected growth and required resources for Extended Instructional Programs, Independent Study, and Capstone Summer Honors Program—all credit programs administered by the Office of Instructional Services for the Division of Continuing Education. In particular, the previous pattern of growth for Extended Instructional Programs had been dramatic and was expected to continue.

In 1971, fewer than 300 students had taken advantage of alternative methods of instruction by registering for courses through Extended Instructional Programs. In 1972 the figure increased to approximately 1,000 and by 1978 there had been close to 3,000 registrations. Growth was expected to increase as off-campus programs and Weekend College continued to attract the part-time, adult student.

Figure 1. Projected Enrollment in Office of Extended Programs

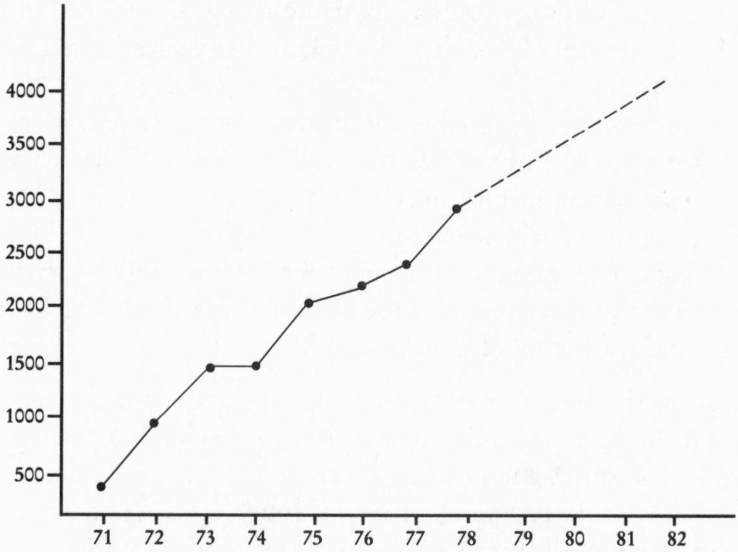

Five-Year Goals, 1978–1983

Given this pattern of growth and the anticipated level of continued growth, goals for Extended Instructional Programs for the next five years included broadening, expanding, and improving the quality of the ongoing educational alternatives offered for the non-traditional student. It was expected that this could be achieved by the following:

* developing additional offerings through off-campus programs, and Weekend College;
* increasing the number and type of individual courses offered off-campus, on weekends and through Independent Study; offerings in Commerce and Business Administration, Education, Communications, Social Work, Arts and Sciences, and Nursing were to be added;
* increasing faculty participation in developing, teaching and communicating about the office's credit programs through workshops and presentations at departmental meetings;
* identifying types of credit programs currently needed by non-traditional students by conducting surveys and increasing involvement with the University's Regional Offices;
* improving the quality of instruction in Independent Study, off-campus classes, and Weekend College by sponsoring faculty development programs, with attention to delivery using multimedia devices;
* establishing a marketing and promotional office to assist various departments of the Division with the promotion and marketing of their programs.

Also, the five-year plan included working with the academic units and administrative offices to develop University-wide procedures and policies which would recognize faculty participation in programs offered through Instructional Services as part of the reward systems for promotion, tenure, and salary. The plan called for creation of an office to serve as a contact point within the University for credit and non-credit students.

Planners also proposed expanding the experiential learning activities of regular students by assuming responsibility for coordination of the University's Interim Program, which would involve placements in national, state, and local agencies. An Alumni College was also proposed to operate in conjunction with the Capstone Summer Honors Program. It would operate during the regular summer term and offer alumni the opportunity to return to campus to participate in academically stimulating activities.

Other initiatives put forth for 1978–83 included increasing student enrollment in the Capstone Summer Honors Program; improving research opportunities for off-campus, Independent Study, and Weekend College students by making materials more readily available through the five Regional Offices; strengthening staff development programs in the area of grant proposal writing; and working with administrative personnel to develop plans, procedures, and policies for making financial assistance available to qualified adult and part-time students.

The Adult Student Office, 1980

The five-year plan finalized discussions that had begun in 1977 regarding serving the adult part-time student. For some time, continuing education staff and others in the administration had felt the need to create an office designed to serve the adult part-time student.

In the spring of 1977, Dr. Howard Gundy, academic vice-

1978-80

Capstone Summer Honors program initiated by and administered in the Division.

THE ADULT STUDENT OFFICE FUNCTIONED FROM 1980–82 TO SERVE THE
GROWING POPULATION OF ADULT LEARNERS IN ALABAMA. THE OFFICE WAS
REVIVED IN 1985.

president, had requested that the Office of Extended Instructional Programs assume some responsibility for publicizing
the non-traditional credit offerings of The University of Alabama. In response to this request, the office developed a
comprehensive publicity program which included a tabloid
listing of offerings, television and radio public service announcements, and newspaper advertisements.

In 1978, Dr. Bryan proposed that the Division of Continuing Education be the initial contact point for part-time students interested in credit as well as non-credit programs. He
felt that such an office would eliminate the impersonal image
projected by the University to many part-time students. Personnel in the office could serve as brokers, matching individual needs to the many services available on campus.

Responsibilities of the office were to include:

* publicizing the University's evening, off-campus, weekend, independent study, interim term, and summer
  school programs;

* providing a contact point within the University accessible to any potential part-time students;
* assisting part-time students with admission and registration for classes;
* registering part-time students in the evenings prior to the beginning of their first class;
* cataloging the resources of the University and identifying specific individuals in each academic or service area who would respond to inquiries by potential part-time students;
* following up on all requests to ensure than an appropriate response was made to all requests by part-time students;
* keeping records of contacts, recommending new programs, and identifying obstacles within the University that impede adequate service to non-traditional students; and,
* working to eliminate obstacles, identifying new programs or existing programs that need revision.

Typical matters of concern that the Adult Student Office might address could be registration by mail, counseling of students, establishing re-entry programs for adults, developing orientation programs for the part-time student, and working with appropriate University offices to serve students during the lunch hour and at other convenient times.

In his proposal, Dr. Bryan estimated that the costs for such an office could be borne within the Division. By fall of 1980, the Adult Student Office was functioning, with a director and a full-time secretary. Dr. Bryan and his staff made efforts to publicize the office and its services statewide as the point of

---

1980

SAFE STATE ON-SITE CONSULTATION PROGRAM BECOMES A PART OF CONTINUING ENGINEERING EDUCATION.

---

contact with the University for adult students, ages 22 and up. Susan Hathaway served as the first director and was later succeeded by Edward O. Brown. Mr. Brown started an orientation for returning adult students which introduced them to the programs and services of the University. Unfortunately, the Adult Student Office only survived until 1982 when it fell victim to proration. (It was revived in 1986 under Dean Dennis P. Prisk.)

The Adult Student Office, like Weekend College and the proposed Summer Inter-Session, acknowledged the demographic trend toward part-time adult students and took the initiative in communicating with people who made up the widening circle of non-traditional University students.

High School Programs and Capstone Summer Honors Program

The Extension Division, Extended Services, and, in Dr. Bryan's era, the Division of Continuing Studies had continually offered programs geared toward high school teachers and students. In 1978, at the urging of Dr. Gundy, the Division initiated the Capstone Summer Honors Program. Some of the principal benefits of the program as envisioned by Dr. Gundy were the increase in the cultural, recreational, and informational opportunities for all of the University's summer students.

In January 1980, however, direct responsibility for the Capstone Summer Honors Program was moved to the Office of Admission Services. In May 1981, Dr. Bryan communicated to Dr. E. Roger Sayers, academic vice-president, his belief that

---

1980

THE OFFICE OF ADULT STUDENTS OPENS BUT IS CUT AFTER TWO YEARS DUE TO PRORATION.

---

the Capstone Summer Honors Program could best be served if it was moved back to Continuing Education. This was not accomplished; however, within Dr. Bryan's proposal was another proposal geared toward secondary students and teachers, the Capstone Spanish Institute, which was acted upon.

The Capstone Spanish Institute, conceived as a joint effort with the Department of Romance Languages and Classics and the Mexico City campus of Instituto Technologico de Monterrey, was housed in the Office of Extended Instructional Programs. The Institute targeted secondary school juniors and Spanish Language teachers from the public and private schools in the state of Alabama. The program was set to begin in June 1983 and was well-marketed statewide. Although it represented an excellent cooperative model between Continuing Education, Arts and Sciences, and an international university and targeted secondary students and teachers in Alabama, the Capstone Spanish Institute drew only a handful of students and teachers. Because of this lack of interest, the Institute could not be held in the summer of 1983, and it was not offered again.

Safe State Consultation Program Becomes Part of Continuing Engineering Education

In 1980, the Safe State On-Site Consultation Program became a part of the Division of Continuing Education. This program was administered by Ray Hollub, who was also in charge of OSHA Training and Continuing Engineering Education. Hollub was named as special assistant to the dean at this time. OSHA contracts for 1981 exceeded $1,700,000.

Continuing Engineering Education provided engineers, technologists, and associated professionals special programs related to interests and needs within the field of engineering. Basic educational goals included giving a better understanding of new technologies, allowing interaction with regulatory

IN 1976, CONTINUING ENGINEERING EDUCATION BEGAN PROVIDING
OCCUPATIONAL SAFETY AND HEALTH (OSHA) INSPECTORS FROM ALL
50 STATES WITH BASIC FOUNDRY TRAINING.

agencies, and ensuring opportunity for professional improvement.

Safe State, begun in 1978, carried out Continuing Engineering Education's mission in a very specialized way by providing a health and safety consultation service to the state of Alabama. The University was the first four-year institution in the United States to be designated by the U.S. Department of

---

1981

DR. JOAB THOMAS BECOMES UNIVERSITY PRESIDENT AND MANDATES A STRONG
CONTINUING EDUCATION PROGRAM.

Labor to provide health and safety consultation services, and it gained a national reputation as such. (It was also the national training center for the U.S. Department of Labor Consultation Program.) Academic institutions in other states followed in the footsteps of the University to provide consultation services to business and industry.

As of 1981, Safe State had provided service to approximately one-half million people in Alabama by serving more than 3,000 business and industries in the state. Its professional consultants (safety specialists and certified industrial hygienists) had identified and effectively removed more than 20,000 workplace hazards.

The Safe State program, while administered in Tuscaloosa, maintained consultants in Decatur, Mobile, and Dothan. The project was funded in part by the Alabama State Legislature to provide similar services to the public sector of Alabama. Activities in 1981 serving the public sector included those with the State Highway Department, school systems throughout the state, the State Docks, and other state agencies.

From 1978-81, the University provided the U.S. Department of Labor with approximately 70,000 contact hours of specialized training for safety and health consultants nationwide. Technical training for safety and health consultants was provided for each state in the nation that had a safety and health consultation program. The off-campus activities in this program included more than 200 presentations conducted at 25 different universities or sites around the United States from 1978-81.

While not an academic program per se, the training programs developed through Continuing Engineering Education had, and continue to have, a high degree of expertise and technological content.

1982

DR. THOMAS BARTLETT NAMED CHANCELLOR OF THE UNIVERSITY OF ALABAMA SYSTEM; SERVES UNTIL 1989.

Ray Hollub

"OF ALL THE WORK I DID, I AM PERHAPS PROUDEST OF A PROGRAM WE RAN FOR SOME 600 NEWLY UNEMPLOYED NASA ENGINEERS. WE PROVIDED THESE PEOPLE WITH JOB PLACEMENT INFORMATION, PSYCHOLOGICAL COUNSELING, AND HOPE TO FACE A COMPETITIVE JOB MARKET AGAIN. THIS ACTIVITY GOT NO PUBLICITY, BUT IT WAS AN ESSENTIAL, TRUE SERVICE."

After an academic career in engineering, Ray Hollub began working for Extended Services in 1971 as director of Continuing Engineering Education in order to develop a program for contract training.

Mr. Hollub lists among significant achievements for the Division the establishment of foundry training for U.S. Department of Labor inspectors. In 1976, after learning that Occupational Safety and Health Administration (OSHA) had "blasted foundries for not protecting safety inspectors," Mr. Hollub wrote to Dr. Morton Corn, U.S. Secretary of Labor, proposing that The University of Alabama provide OSHA inspectors basic foundry training. Three months later, Washington officials came to see UA's foundry and in a year and a half Continuing Engineering Education had trained 600 OSHA inspectors from all 50 states.

This successful partnership led to the eventual development of Safe State, the first university-based on-site consultation service for the U.S. Department of Labor. Though other universities later followed suit, Safe State remained a national model well into the 1990s.

Mr. Hollub led Continuing Engineering Education to a

number of successful contract training programs for government and private industry. Among these was a 1.1-million-dollar contract to help Alabama schools evaluate asbestos contamination in their facilities. This asbestos abatement program became a national model, with all elementary and secondary schools in Alabama becoming virtually asbestos-free in compliance with EPA regulations.

In 1981, Mr. Hollub was named assistant to the dean of the Division of Continuing Education and in 1984 assistant dean for the College of Continuing Studies. He returned to the College of Engineering to head the Aerospace Engineering Department in 1986.

The Division Continues to be Productive with Reduced Staff

In late summer of 1980, Dr. Bryan reported that although positions and salaries had been cut from the Division's budget for the previous three years, the unit had managed to function well as an increasingly "lean administration." Since May 1977, when Dr. Bryan had become dean of the Division, the positions of director of the Metric Institute, director of High School Services, director of Capstone Summer Honors Program, director of Library Services, special assistant to the dean, coordinator of Title I — Small Business, and staff for Civil Defense Training had been discontinued. Dr. Bryan noted that from 1976–77 to 1979–80, CEUs generated had held steady and semester hours had increased substantially.

A year later, Dr. Bryan reported to Dr. Sayers that non-credit contact hour production for adult participants for June 1, 1980—May 31, 1981, was continuing to increase. While there were 235,105 contact hours generated in 1977–78, there were 318,859 in 1980-81. Again, he noted that in this four-year

---

1982

PRORATION RESULTS IN STAFF REDUCTIONS.

---

period there had been a net loss of six professional positions in the non-credit area.

Clearly, Dr. Bryan was making the point that the Division's staff was adapting to available resources and continuing to serve the growing constituencies of continuing education.

Expansion of Non-traditional Degree Opportunities

By 1981, there were eleven degree or certificate programs available to adults through the non-traditional delivery system within the Division of Continuing Education. These included master's degrees in elementary education, early childhood education, secondary education, educational administration, supervision and curriculum development, and vocational industrial education, as well as master's degrees in criminal justice and social work. Certificate programs in audiology (15 undergraduate semester hours) and archaeology (18 undergraduate semester hours), and a specialist in gerontology (15 semester graduate hours) were offered.

Two areas considered for expansion at this time were Industrial Hygiene (the closest degree program being at the University of Oklahoma) and degrees that might be completed in conjunction with CUUP (Cooperative University Upper Division Program) in Gadsden.

A degree in general studies housed within the Division of Continuing Education was considered because it might permit the needed flexibility. However, after extensive study it was decided that rather than propose a non-traditional degree for Continuing Education, a better course would be to request a cooperative arrangement with New College. With New College's commitment to students who showed serious motivation toward earning a degree independently, it seemed that New College could best assist the Division of Continuing Education in meeting the needs of all adult learners.

New College and Continuing Education began working together to implement the External Degree program through CUUP. Teams from New College held orientations for the program in Gadsden, and then Gadsden staff served as liaison between New College External Degree students in the Gadsden area and the main campus, advising and helping coordinate out-of-class-learning contracts for Gadsden-area students. Working closely with New College, the Gadsden Center thus facilitated the New College External Degree program until CUUP was discontinued in 1986.

Cooperative Programs with Auburn University to Train Secondary Teachers and Administrators

In July 1972, the presidents of Auburn University and The University of Alabama had both endorsed an agreement to cooperatively offer graduate courses off-campus and for students of both institutions to attend courses. Dr. L. Tennent Lee, who at that time was assigned responsibility for all University off-campus courses, assisted with the administration of this from Tuscaloosa.

In 1976, a proposal for annual orientations and support seminars for public education leadership personnel in Alabama was drawn up by both universities. Within the Division of Continuing Education, Dr. Lanny Gamble and J. Foster Watkins spearheaded the effort. Programs were held each year through 1982.

In 1981–82, a schedule was drawn up between The University of Alabama and Auburn University providing for several joint programs between the two institutions that would serve the needs of Alabama's secondary school teachers and administrators. Historically, both Auburn University and The University of Alabama had had a profound effect on the elemen-

---

1983

PRESIDENT THOMAS ANNOUNCES UNIVERSITY PLANS TO BUILD A CONTINUING EDUCATION COMPLEX, INCLUDING A CONFERENCE CENTER AND HOTEL, THE PAUL W. BRYANT MUSEUM, AND AN ALUMNI HALL.

---

tary and secondary school teachers and administrators in the state. As the only terminal-degree-granting institutions for graduate study of education in Alabama, both institutions had also worked closely with the State Department of Education. Now, both institutions were interested in working together to help improve Alabama's schools by offering their teachers and administrators both pre- and in-service training in this joint initiative.

A master's degree for school administrators—through the Area of Administration and Planning for the College of Education—was planned, with course work for this program happening at Ann Jordan Lodge and selected courses being taught on campus in Auburn and Tuscaloosa. The program would be offered primarily on weekends to permit full-time employed school personnel to participate.

Also, in-service courses for new superintendents of education as well as staff development seminars at Ann Jordan Lodge for school teachers and administrators were planned for summer 1981 and summer 1982.

Both of these programs arose from concerns that there was a shortage of appropriately trained school principals in the state of Alabama. Officials on both campuses felt that this shortage would worsen as new certification standards requiring in-field employment might discourage potential school principals from seeking graduate degrees in school administration without some assurance that they would be placed in an administrative position. Also, it was felt that the new certification guideline requiring school principals to be certified at either the elementary, middle school, or secondary-level would further delimit placement possibilities of current school principals.

This cooperative program among the two institutions and the State Department of Education represented an effort to improve the educational system of the state. Although it was a modest program, it did serve as a model for further cooperative efforts.

JOAB L. THOMAS

Dr. Joab L. Thomas Named University President, 1981

On July 1, 1981, Dr. Joab L. Thomas assumed the presidency of The University of Alabama. Included in Dr. Thomas's vision for the direction of the University was a mandate for a vital, forward-looking continuing education program. Dr. Thomas realized the potential for The University of Alabama to serve more fully the burgeoning market for continuing higher education. His support of continuing education in general, and his spearheading of the drive to build the Bryant Conference Center and Hotel complex (which would be officially announced in 1983) were key factors in the evolution of the contemporary College of Continuing Studies.

Continuing Education Consortium Established with the University, University of Southern Mississippi, and Mississippi State University, 1981

Following discussions among representatives from the University of Southern Mississippi, Mississippi State Univer-

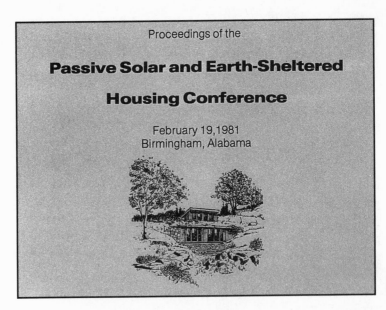

sity, and The University of Alabama in August 1981, an agreement was signed establishing a Continuing Education Consortium among the three campuses. The Consortium's role and scope included better serving the needs and interests of non-traditional learners in the Alabama/Mississippi area by jointly sponsoring conference activities, sharing independent study materials, securing resource people, and conducting professional development activities for Continuing Education staff. In addition, the three institutions planned to cooperate in a foreign and domestic travel program, develop grant proposals, and provide consultative technical assistance to business, industry, and government through programs of the Consortium.

Quarterly meetings facilitated ongoing Consortium programs and activities and were set to happen in January, April, July, and October in Meridian. Each institution had a designated contact person and budgets were developed jointly. The detailed Consortium agreement spelled out marketing concerns, other benefits, and the need to address program planning, coordination, and evaluation.

Some of the 1981 programs which the Consortium mounted included a "Passive Solar and Earth-Sheltered Housing" workshop held at the University, a program called "Discipline Techniques and Procedures: Teacher Liability" set for Jackson and Montgomery which was cancelled, and a Bass Institute for which MSU served as lead institution with Indiana State University participating via contract.

Ann Jordan Retreat in 1982 Nets New Proposals, Plans

After returning from a working retreat with Division staff at Ann Jordan Lodge in late summer 1982, Dr. Bryan reported a summary of announcements and comments, some of which held long-range significance.

Once again, the Continuing Education Center took top billing. Dr. Bryan reported that the consulting firm of Laventhol and Horwath was making a feasibility study and involving Division staff as well as faculty who had been involved in programs.

During the meeting, one of the groups had discussed long- and short-range plans for the Center; another brainstormed the best organization possible for the Division; and a third group considered income, self-support, overhead, and profit-sharing ideas. The need for increased marketing and promotion came up several times and coincided with Dr. Bryan's previously expressed desire to established an office for this purpose.

These discussions were significant because reorganization of the Division would occur in the coming years; preparing for the Bryant Conference Center and Hotel would require tremendous time and energy on the part of the continuing education staff and would impact program planning; and marketing, promotion, and communication—especially through targeted direct mail marketing—would require more resources and expertise in future years.

Participants at the 5th Annual Mining Conference, April 1982, viewed an exhibit of the latest mining equipment.

News broadcaster Herb Kaplow (L) met with summer honors program participants in summer 1978.

Status of the Division in 1982–1983

The 1982–83 academic year would be Dr. Bryan's last year as dean of the Division of Continuing Education. During this time Dr. Bryan communicated to Dr. Sayers and others the Division's commitment to providing quality programming in the face of the effects of proration and the weak economy. Traditional or recurring programs managed to thrive despite cutbacks and exciting, new initiatives were on the table.

In several reports, Dr. Bryan articulated the current and projected status of the Division. As he did, he cited high-quality, on-going programs which had been held during 1982–83:

* the 16th Alabama Industrial Development Conference, sponsored by the University and the Industrial Developers Association of Alabama;
* the 36th Federal Tax Clinic, designed to update accountants and attorneys on current tax regulations;
* the 68th and 69th Semi-annual CPA Review Courses, a nationally recognized program held in the fall and spring each year;
* the 5th Annual Mining Institute, a program of national stature, with proceedings distributed worldwide in 1982;
* the 10th Symposium on English and American Literature, which brought national and international scholars to campus;
* Continuing Legal Education, offering annual seminars in banking law, corporate law, and estate planning as well as the Southeastern Trial Institute, a Recent Developments Seminar, and more than 50 one-day seminars of interest to Alabama attorneys;
* the 34th Church Music Workshop, designed to help the practicing church musician sharpen skills and learn new techniques.

CCS

UA PRESIDENT DAVID MATTHEWS WITH GADSDEN CENTER COOPERATIVE UPPER
DIVISION GRADUATE MARGARET COURAN, CIRCA 1980.

Programs in Response to Current Needs

In addition to the traditional and recurring programs, others had been developed in response to particular needs of adult
learners. In discussing the status of the Division, Dr. Bryan
highlighted new programs in 1981–82 which came about in
response to such needs. Some of these included a conference
on black stress, which received an NUCEA Creative Programming Award; the Passive Solar and Earth-Sheltered
Housing Conference that resulted from the Consortium with
the University of Southern Mississippi and Mississippi State
University; and the Advanced Placement Institute for high
school teachers (which continues in the 1990s). In addition, a
first-of-its-kind Mine Ventilation Symposium drew an international audience; a conference on "Children and Death: The
Impact on Families and Community Systems" was co-sponsored with the College of Community Health Sciences; and
the English Language Institute was initiated to offer intensive
English language study and cultural orientation to students,
businessmen, and preparing professional for further study in
the United States.

Also during this time, Independent Study established a certificate program in Criminal Justice that consisted of thirty semester hours.

OSHA Consultation Training Program and Safe State Consultation Program

In 1982, the training component of the OSHA Consultation Training Program served 46 states. Safe State, the confidential safety and health consulting service for Alabama, was also operated through the Division. The 1981–82 budget for the two activities totaled $1.25 million. Additional funding that was projected to reach $1.1 million during 1983 had been committed by the state to enable Safe State to assist with the asbestos removal program in local school systems. Already a national leader, the University was destined to have a national impact on work place health and safety.

Southeastern Training Center for Cooperative Education Established by Federal Grant

Also significant at this time was the fact that Cooperative Education received a $106,300 grant from the U.S. Department of Education for the establishment of the Southeastern Training Center for Cooperative Education. This program would prove to be ongoing for at least ten more years and provided important service to cooperative education specialists throughout a large part of the United States by hosting conferences and workshops in the area of cooperative education.

Future Plans: 1982–1983

The Division staff planned to sponsor the Advanced Placement Institutes again in 1982–83, host a math institute in cooperation with the colleges of Education and Arts and Sciences, and host two Book Arts Institutes, among others. The Law Enforcement Academy had put a proposal on the table to establish a Law Enforcement Training and Research Center that would better serve the law enforcement community. Finally, it was noted that the necessary equipment had been secured to begin training programs in Computer-Assisted Instruction in fall 1982 at the Gadsden Center.

The Division was also involved in contract and grant activity that totalled close to 1.4 million dollars in 1981–82, almost 15 percent of the total amount of contract and grant monies generated by the University.

While programs proceeded and plans were in the works for program growth, staff reorganization, computer-updating, and even building a conference center, Dr. Bryan was compelled to conclude in some of his written communications that the Division still had obstacles to overcome, some of which were simply beyond its control, such as the poor state of the U.S. economy. Barriers to the enrollment of adult students still apparently existed, though he noted that the Adult Student Enrollment Committee would possibly help on this score.

Also, Dr. Bryan felt that there continued to be a helpful spirit of cooperation among the University's academic deans. He hoped for even greater involvement of University faculty in exploring new ways to serve the adult population and to improve ways of program delivery. Dr. Bryan also felt that the Division should assume a more effective role in providing

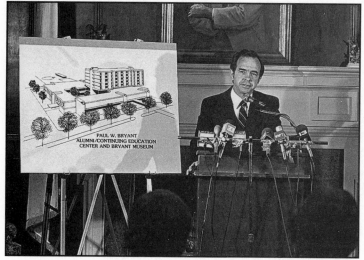

UNIVERSITY RELATIONS

PRESIDENT THOMAS HELD A NEWS CONFERENCE IN FEBRUARY 1983 TO UNVEIL
PLANS FOR THE PAUL W. BRYANT ALUMNI/CONTINUING EDUCATION CENTER
AND BRYANT MUSEUM.

liaison among divisions of the University in the development
of interdisciplinary programs. He cited the proposed Center
for Law Enforcement Research and Service as an example of
this. Building on the Basic Academy, it would be possible to
involve as many as five academic divisions in a program to
provide training, research, and service to the law enforcement
profession. The safety and health training and consultation
program also offered a great opportunity for growth as other
parts of the University became involved, he concluded.

Continuing Education Complex Announced in
February 1983

On February 3, 1983, President Thomas announced plans
for an $11-million facility—the Paul W. Bryant Alumni/Con-
tinuing Education Center and Bryant Museum. The 100,000-
square-foot complex, to be built on the University's east
campus across from Memorial Coliseum, would "serve as the

focal point for alumni activities, adult learning and off-campus services of the University by bringing all those programs under one roof," Dr. Thomas said.

The Paul W. Bryant Museum was planned to house memorabilia of Coach Bryant and the teams he coached. Dr. Thomas had discussed the plans with Coach Bryant, who was aware that the complex would be named in his honor, and he had expressed his appreciation to Dr. Thomas for that.

In announcing the facility, Dr. Thomas said that the first phase of the building would be funded by a campaign with a $5 million goal. This would underwrite construction of conference rooms, offices, dining rooms, and other facilities for continuing education, and office space and meeting rooms for alumni and the alumni office staff.

The second building phase would involve the private construction and management of guest accommodations. At that time, Phase I was scheduled to begin in 1984 and Phase II the following year. As it turned out, the Sheraton Capstone Inn opened in December of 1986 with the Paul W. Bryant Conference Center and Alumni Hall opening the following October, in 1987.

According to Dr. Thomas, the facility illustrated the University's concerted effort to meet the needs of "higher education's fastest growing clientele—the adult learner." Bringing the continuing education and alumni staffs physically closer together was also seen as a means of increasing alumni involvement in continuing education.

"To fulfill our mission as a comprehensive university, we are challenged to improve the quality and increase the variety of programs offered to adults, and this facility is essential to that task," Dr. Thomas said.

The facilities proposed at that time in an architect's rendering showed the complex as one contained facility. The final complex would include four free-standing buildings connected by walkways.

The University and President Thomas's commitments to

build this complex would change the direction of continuing education for the University and the state of Alabama in many ways. Having a state-of-the-art facility in Tuscaloosa meant that literally any continuing education event could be held on campus and accommodate all facets of a program, from conference rooms equipped with the latest media equipment to executive suite accommodations. The long-held dream of a building designed for, and solely dedicated to, continuing education at The University of Alabama was becoming a reality.

Dr. Bryan Becomes Part-time Assistant to the Academic Vice-President, 1983

In early fall of 1983, Dr. Bryan left the Division of Continuing Education and began working as part-time assistant to the academic vice-president (at that time Dr. Sayers). During 1983–84, he worked to build bridges between the University and the public school systems in the state. Dr. Bryan officially retired in 1984, and continued in a part-time capacity in the Office of Academic Affairs.

CHAPTER 7

PROGRAMMING AND FACILITIES COME OF AGE

Era of Dr. Dennis P. Prisk, 1983–1989

Interim Term of Dr. Robert W. Hudson, 1989–1990

I n the fall of 1983, the Division of Continuing Education stood poised for a major move toward becoming a fully up-to-date, contemporary continuing education unit that would best extend the resources of The University of Alabama to a broad range of adult learners. Dr. Dennis P. Prisk, former associate dean of the School of Continuing Studies for the Indiana University System, was named dean of the Division in October 1983. Shortly thereafter the Division became the College of Continuing Studies and took its place among the other major academic units on campus.

Among the major items on Dr. Prisk's agenda were revamping the organizational structure of the College; initiating program development in all credit and non-credit areas; overseeing the building of the Bryant Conference Center and Hotel complex and developing the facilities in Martha Parham West to their fullest; creating a sound fiscal base for the College; and automating the College's systems, particularly computerization of the College's registration services, program fiscal tracking, and graphics department, among others. Though a number of other challenges presented themselves during Dr. Prisk's tenure as dean, these were the five major areas on which he and his staff concentrated from 1983–89.

The developments in the College of Continuing Studies

University Relations

Dr. Dennis P. Prisk

during this time coincided with President Thomas's desire to revitalize The University of Alabama as a major research institution. A contemporary continuing education unit, fully staffed, well-equipped, and with state-of-the-art facilities at its disposal, could best serve the University's mission.

Organizational Changes within the College

Shortly after arriving on campus, Dr. Prisk reviewed the organization of the Division of Continuing Education, and suggested that as a College of Continuing Studies certain programs and directions should be discontinued while other areas should be either expanded or created anew.

Offices that were phased out included Conference Activities, Continuing Education in Human Resources, Program Development, Ann Jordan Lodge, Special Adult Studies, and Alabama Recreation and Parks Society. Numerous long-standing programs facilitated by Conference Activities were to be administered by the newly formed Division of Profes-

---

1983

Dr. Dennis P. Prisk named dean of College of Continuing Studies.

---

sional and Special Programs (which later became Division of Professional and Management Development Programs). The thrust of this reorganization was to shift toward professional updating or management-oriented courses, seminars, and workshops (and away from leisure-learning courses of any type). Also, increased credit opportunities were explored and new off-campus degree programs put in place, such as the Maxwell Air Force Base master's and Ph.D programs. While leisure learning had certainly not dominated the activities of extension and continuing education at any point in its history at the University, it's accurate to say that the coming of age of continuing education at the University would require that resources be focused on programs that targeted the adult student returning to college for a degree or the working professional seeking to upgrade or enhance skills, rather than toward the casual learner.

From 1983 until 1986, in addition to the existing divisions of the College which included Office of the Dean, Law Enforcement Academy, Independent Study Division, Cooperative Education Program/Southeastern Training Center, and the Child Development Associate Training Program, five new divisions were established. In 1984, the Office of Budget and Planning and the Office of Marketing and Communications were created. In 1985, two more service-oriented offices came into being: the Adult Student Office and the Office of College Relations. And in 1986, the Division of Environmental and Industrial Programs was created through a merger of Continuing Engineering Education, OSHA training programs, and Safe State.

The positions of associate dean and assistant dean were created as part of the reorganization. In 1983, Roy Watford was named associate dean and served in this capacity until 1985. In 1984, Ray Hollub, director of Continuing Engineering Education and assistant to the dean, was appointed assistant dean of Continuing Studies. Prof. Hollub returned to the College of Engineering in 1986. In 1985, Dr. Robert B. Leiter, formerly director of the Division of Special Programs, Eastern Kentucky University, was named associate dean of Continuing Studies.

Administratively, Dr. Leiter was responsible for five divisions of the College: the Adult Student Office, the Office of Budget and Planning, the Gadsden Center, the Bryant Conference Center and Hotel, and the Office of Marketing and Communications. From summer 1986 through summer 1987, Dr. Leiter was acting director of the Office of Marketing and Communications.

Office of Budget and Planning

The charge of the Office of Budget and Planning was to ensure that the College managed its financial resources as effectively as possible. Dr. Prisk felt that good financial management was even more critical than ever in view of the fact that the College was required to generate approximately 80 percent of its budget through income.

From 1983–85, the Office of Budget and Planning coordinated the automating of the College's systems, assuring that each department was equipped with personal computers, printers, and software compatible with other departments in the College. In addition, a mini-main-frame computer—the IBM System 36—was installed, dedicated primarily to functioning as a common database for the divisions, as a window to the University's administrative mainframe, and also for the automation of record-keeping functions of the Independent Study Division.

In addition, the Office acquired a conference budgeting program for personal computers and trained College staff on the use of that program to project anticipated revenue, expen-

---

1983–84

The Division of Continuing Education becomes the College of Continuing Studies; reorganization of program units.

Dr. Minnie Miles was honored in 1986 for her work as founder of the Women in Management Conference.

In 1987, Atlanta mayor Andrew Young spoke at the Historically and Predominantly Black Colleges and Universities Conference held in Atlanta.

In 1987, UA president Dr. Joab Thomas [left] and Continuing Studies dean Dr. Dennis Prisk [right] accepted a check from Doris Trimm of Birmingham to establish the Hershel Trimm Memorial Endowed Scholarship Fund, the first such fund designated for adult students at the University.

AUTOMATION OF THE COLLEGE'S SYSTEMS, SUCH AS ACCOUNTING, REGISTRATION, MAILING LISTS, WORD PROCESSING, AND GRAPHIC DESIGN MEANT GREATER EFFICIENCY AND PROVIDED OPPORTUNITIES FOR GROWTH.

ditures, and break-even points for future non-credit conferences and seminars. It also automated the College's annual
budget process using personal computers and spreadsheet
software. Mailing lists, previously maintained on a University
mainframe system, were converted to a mailing list package on
the System 36, thus allowing marketing professionals within
the College easier access to list counts and production of labels
on quick turn-around. By 1988, the Office had facilitated the
development of a comprehensive registration software package for non-credit offerings by the College.

In general, the Office of Budget and Planning also helped
establish a sound fiscal base for the College, thus making
future projections more reliable.

The Office of Marketing and Communications

To centralize the marketing function of the College, Dr.
Prisk established the Office of Marketing and Communica-

GINNY GANONG NICHOLS, MONTAGE STUDIO INC.

THE DIRECT MAIL FUNCTION OF THE COLLEGE WAS ENHANCED BY THE ADVENT OF DESKTOP PUBLISHING, ALLOWING HIGH QUALITY ARTWORK AT A REASONABLE COST.

tions in January 1984. The office was conceived as an in-house advertising agency for the College to efficiently promote the activities of the program units to targeted markets. While direct mailings had been used for many years in extension and continuing education as the primary means of communicating

1983

MAXWELL AIRFORCE BASE MASTER OF ARTS IN MILITARY HISTORY BEGINS.

with potential attendees, the Office was able to modernize this operation by eventually organizing all in-house mailing lists on the System 36 and publishing a mailing list directory for use within the College.

The Office was staffed in 1984 with a director, a part-time graphic designer, and one support staff member. As demands for the services of the department grew, writer/editors, more graphic support, account executives, and a mailing list coordinator were added. Desk-top publishing computer equipment aided the Office in producing top-quality print pieces to reach the wide variety of constituents that the College served. Centralized publicity efforts, also initiated in 1985, resulted in increased local and regional news coverage for College events. By 1989, the Office was fully serving all program units of the College, handling direct mail projects in excess of $400,000.

Tracking direct mail marketing efforts was initiated in 1985 so that subsequent mailing list purchases and other marketing budgetary decisions could be made wisely. All direct mail marketing of non-credit programs was tracked on a regular basis from 1985 and continues presently. Credit programs and other marketing efforts were, and continue to be, tracked also.

The Adult Student Office

In 1985, the Adult Student Office was opened to serve the increasing population of adults returning to campus or entering college for the first time. (This office marked a return to providing service that was offered from 1980–82 for adults.) The Adult Student Office served as a point of entry to the University for anyone over 25, offering a variety of information such as how to register, obtain financial aid, or use other services of the University. A support group called EASE

1983

COMPUTERIZATION OF THE COLLEGE'S SYSTEMS BEGINS; MOST SYSTEMS IN PLACE BY 1985.

ADULT STUDENTS MEET AT THE NOON HOUR IN THE SUPPORT GROUP EASE (ENRICHING THE ADULT STUDENT ENVIRONMENT) IN ORDER TO SHARE THEIR EXPERIENCES AS ADULTS RETURNING TO COLLEGE OR ENTERING FOR THE fiRST TIME.

(Enriching the Adult Student Environment), begun in 1985, met once a week at the noon hour so that adults could get together and share their stories and concerns of returning to college. The Returning Adult Seminar, begun in the summer of 1986 prior to the fall semester, was a free, evening program at which numerous University officials spoke briefly on the services and programs available on campus. In 1987, EASE received a Creative Programming Award from the National University Continuing Education Association.

An additional service provided by the Office included maintaining an adult student resource library and information center adjacent to the Adult Student Office in Martha Parham West. The Adult Student Office and its programs represent the College and the University's commitment to the adult student.

The Office of College Relations

A second service-oriented office, the Office of College Relations, was created within the College in 1985. The Office of College Relations served as a fund-raising facilitator to all divisions of the College for developing and maintaining external sources of funding from foundations, corporations, professional associations, and individuals. The Office also coordi-

THE JOHN G. BURTON
ENDOWMENT FOR THE SUPPORT OF
MUNICIPAL PROGRAMS HONORS
MR. BURTON AND IS ONE OF THE
COLLEGE OF CONTINUING
STUDIES' SCHOLARSHIP EFFORTS
WHICH MAKES CONTINUING
EDUCATION FOR MUNICIPAL
EMPLOYEES AND THEIR TRAINING
PROGRAMS POSSIBLE.

nated research and contract activities and fostered effective public relations for the College.

From 1985–87, the Office was instrumental in establishing several adult student scholarships including the Hershell Trimm Memorial Endowed Scholarship, a general scholarship for an adult student in financial need; the Samuel Howard Endowed Scholarship for incarcerated persons wanting to continue their education through Independent Study; and, the John G. Burton Endowment for the Support of Municipal Programs. The Clarice Parker Memorial Endowed Scholarship was established in 1988 with funds from the estate of Ms. Parker, a long-time extension employee and former director of Independent Study.

Financial Reorganization

Dr. Prisk's reorganization of the College extended to finances as well. In 1983, the College was financially reorganized

1984

PROFESSIONAL DEVELOPMENT COURSES ARE INITIATED.

to clearly establish cost and profit centers. The offices that did not generate income were defined as cost centers. These included the Dean's office, Office of Budget and Planning, Office of Marketing and Communications, Adult Student Office, and Cooperative Education. The College's "hard money" allocation by the University would support these offices.

Units within the College that did generate revenue were defined as profit centers. These units included the Divisions of Environmental and Industrial Programs, Professional and Management Development Programs, Instructional Programs, and Independent Study, as well as the Office of College Relations, Law Enforcement Academy, and Paul W. Bryant Conference Center.

In addition to University general fund allocations and earned income, the College's other sources of funds were contracts and grants and gift funds. For the fiscal year ending September 30, 1987, funding sources were divided fairly evenly among earned income—non-credit (27.95%), credit (22.90%)—contracts and grants (27.45%), and the University's allocation (20.98%). Gift funds at that time made up less than one percent.

Non-Credit Program Development

In 1984, annual programs and conferences from several areas were shifted to the newly created Division of Professional Development Programs and Division of Management Development Programs, both staffed by program managers and support staff, with one director administering both divisions. With the arrival of a new director in 1985, the two divisions were combined and called the Division of Professional and Management Development Programs.

1984

MAXWELL AIR FORCE BASE DOCTORATE IN PUBLIC ADMINISTRATION BEGINS.

GINNY GANONG NICHOLS, MONTAGE STUDIO INC.

NON-CREDIT PROGRAMMING GREW RAPIDLY FROM 1983–89, WITH EMPHASIS ON
PROFESSIONAL DEVELOPMENT AND MANAGEMENT COURSES,
SEMINARS, AND WORKSHOPS.

From this point on, the Division rapidly increased its program activity in the area of management programs offered for
large and small businesses. Typical workshops included
"Telemarketing," "Motivating Employees for Increased Productivity," and "Understanding and Using Financial State-
ments." Programs geared toward nurses and other health
professionals were also developed; these included a Listen to
the Experts nursing series designed in conjunction with the
Capstone College of Nursing ("Nurse-Physician Communication" and "Ethics in Nursing Practice" were two typical
programs). A wide variety of computer training courses made
use of the College's computer laboratory, installed in 1985.
The area of professional development in general included such
workshops as "Writing for Professional Publication," "Lis-

1984

OFFICE OF BUDGET AND PLANNING ESTABLISHED.

tening and Communicating Skills," and "The Expert Witness and Courtroom Testimony." Many of these programs, and similar ones in the Division of Professional and Management Development, are still popular today.

During Dr. Prisk's tenure as dean, the College continued to sponsor a number of long-term continuing education conferences, more than any other institution in the state. As noted in a 1988 summary report, these included:

* Federal Tax Clinic—41 years
* Southeast Transportation and Distribution Forum—28 years
* Human Resources Management Conference—33 years
* Real Estate Salesmanship Conference—32 years
* Institute for Personnel in Employment Security (IAPES)—32 years
* CPA Review Course—42 years (94 sessions)
* Right of Way Conference—28 years
* Municipal Revenue Officers Conference—19 years
* Surveying and Mapping Conference—20 years
* Southeast Natural Gas Distribution Short Course—18 years
* Municipal Management Training Institute for City Clerks and Administrators—21 years

All of these conferences continue to be staples of College programming.

Credit Programs

The Division of Instructional Programs continued to carry out its mission of developing a comprehensive program of credit opportunities for the full-time working adult. From 1983 to 1988, credit enrollments increased 14.1 percent. By 1988, the Division sponsored programs in conjunction with five other academic units on campus, offering a variety of master's- and doctoral-level programs.

STUDENTS IN THE MASTER OF FINE ARTS IN THEATRE PROGRAM AT THE ALABAMA SHAKESPEARE FESTIVAL HAVE THE RARE OPPORTUNITY TO WORK AS EQUITY ACTORS, AND GAIN OTHER PROFESSIONAL THEATRE EXPERIENCE, WHILE THEY EARN THEIR DEGREES.

In 1985, in conjunction with the College of Arts and Sciences, the Division began sponsoring a master of fine arts in theatre at the Alabama Shakespeare Festival in Montgomery. Students in this innovative program spend all, or a majority, of their period of study in Montgomery working as professional actors, and stage managers, or in other theater-professional capacities.

A master of science degree in criminal justice, designed for practitioners and offered in concentrated sessions on campus, continues to thrive and attract participants from across the country.

Also in conjunction with Arts and Sciences, the College of Continuing Studies began offering two graduate programs at

---

1984

OFFICE OF MARKETING AND COMMUNICATIONS CREATED TO HANDLE ALL PRINT AND BROADCAST ADVERTISING WITHIN THE COLLEGE, AS WELL AS TO UPDATE THE DIRECT MAIL EFFORT.

MAJOR MICHAEL RITZ
PLANNED TO WRITE
HISTORICAL SCREENPLAYS
AFTER EARNING A
MASTER'S IN MILITARY
HISTORY FROM THE
UNIVERSITY OF
ALABAMA THROUGH THE
MAXWELL AIR FORCE
BASE PROGRAM.

JEANIE THOMPSON

Maxwell Air Force Base in Montgomery. In 1983, a master of arts in military history was inaugurated; in 1984, a doctorate program in public administration was begun. Both programs, which continue to do well, attract a wide range of military personnel, many of whom are faculty and students from the Air War College and Air Command and Staff College, as well as state government employees. The programs are two of the largest graduate programs in the College of Arts and Sciences.

Other ongoing programs in place by 1988 that the Division of Instructional Programs sponsored jointly with the College of Education were master of arts programs in Early Childhood Education, Elementary Education, Secondary Education, Educational Administration, and Instructional Leadership at the Gadsden Center and Weekend College. "A" and "AA" certification was offered in each of these.

Beginning in 1983, the Advanced Placement Institute offered high school teachers of advanced placement courses the opportunity to learn new teaching methods and work with peer teachers. This program was offered in conjunction with both the College of Education and the College of Arts and Sciences. In 1986, the AP Institute had 445 teachers attending, the largest enrollment in the nation. In 1987, the College Board recognized the Division of Instructional Programs with its "Outstanding Contribution to the Advanced Placement Program" for the AP Institutes. Physics and math institutes for teachers were also offered in similar formats.

Other graduate programs that the Division co-sponsored included five core courses of the master of library service degree in partnership with the Graduate School of Library Service (in Birmingham and Huntsville) and the master of social work degree, offered in 1987 through Weekend College in conjunction with the School of Social Work. In conjunction with the Office of Rural Services, the College of Arts and Sciences, and the College of Education, the Division offered approximately 20 courses on campus in the Program for Academic and Cultural Enhancement of Rural Schools (PAC-ERS). Finally, the Division supervised growth of the Child Development Associate Training Program (CDA) beginning in 1989.

Division of Environmental and Industrial Programs

In 1986, the Division of Environmental and Industrial Programs was created by combining Continuing Engineering Education, the OSHA training programs, and the Safe State On-Site Consultation Program. The Division's stated mission was to provide University-based training, research, and assistance designed to meet workplace needs in the a variety of areas in engineering, applied science, industrial technology, energy, occupational safety and health, environmental con-

---

1985

ADULT STUDENT OFFICE OPENS TO SERVE AS AN INTER-UNIVERSITY NETWORKING SYSTEM TO ASSIST ADULT STUDENTS.

---

trol, and other technical areas related to regulatory compliance, loss control, productivity, economic growth and development, and technology transfer.

Safe State, founded in late 1977, had helped Alabama employers identify and voluntarily correct 3,824 safety or health hazards in the workplace in 1986. These corrections removed 2,355 workers from direct exposure to these hazards. Industries using this service reported reductions of 50 percent or more in workman's compensation costs, worker injuries, and lost workdays. Demand for Safe State services continued to increase during this period as employers attempted to comply with federal Right-to-Know regulations.

From its inception, the Division of Environmental and Industrial Programs initiated a number of innovative programs, including the Governor's Labor-Management Conference, a CAD/CAM computer technology workshop, a Computer Modeling and Simulation workshop, and a course in developing management skills for engineers. In a summary report published in early 1988, it was noted that the opportunities for growth in this Division were outstanding in the areas of workplace safety, asbestos abatement, health and hazardous materials/waste management, and related areas.

Contract Training

As business, industry, and government leaders sought ways to provide on-site training as an economical alternative to sending individuals to courses away from the workplace, contract training opportunities for the College grew. The Division of Professional and Management Development Pro-

1985

OFFICE OF COLLEGE RELATIONS ESTABLISHED AS THE FUND-RAISING FACILITATOR TO ALL UNITS OF THE COLLEGE. CAPSTONE LIFELONG LEARNING SOCIETY SET UP SHORTLY THEREAFTER.

grams and the Division of Environmental and Industrial Programs cultivated a number of these training contracts from 1983–88. These programs were fiscally advantageous for the College because they did not involve marketing costs. Clients from this period included Gulf States Steel, Kimberly-Clark, Drummond Coal, Jim Walters Corporation, Russell Corporation, Alabama Power Company, Monsanto, JVC, Ciba-Geigy, Alabama National Guard, DCH Regional Medical Center, and Allied Paper Corporation, among others. This type of on-site training, referred to as "tailor-made training" continues to be an important part of the College's mission.

* * * * *

By 1988, Dr. Prisk and his staff of directors in the College were satisfied that the College of Continuing Studies had improved its existing inventory of programs, penetrated new markets, recaptured neglected or slipping markets, and in general, repositioned itself firmly in the state and regional marketplace.

Cooperative Education and the Southeastern Training Center

Between 1983 and 1988, the Cooperative Education Program experienced growth to a level of 300 students per year. Initiatives accomplished during that time included a graduate co-op program, a nursing co-op program, and initiation and co-sponsorship of the University's Career Fairs where students meet a wide variety of potential employers in an exhibit format. In addition, the Cooperative Education Program received ABET (American Board of Engineering Technology) accreditation for its engineering co-op program and continued to administer a growing intern program for political science students in Washington, D.C., and Montgomery, Alabama.

In 1985, the Southeastern Training Center for Cooperative Education—also administered out of the Cooperative Education office—offered the first annual Historically and Predominantly Black Colleges and Universities (HPBCU) cooperative education conference. Held in Winston-Salem, North Carolina, and sponsored by a grant from the U.S. Department of Education, this meeting provided an opportunity for cooperative education professionals from HPBCUs to meet with each other and co-op employers to discuss the unique needs of co-op students at HPBCUs. The following year, at the 1986 HPBCU conference in Atlanta, Georgia, Mrs. Coretta Scott King and Mayor Andrew Young of Atlanta addressed the conferees. This conference continues to be held each year and provides an important service for co-op programs at HPBCUs.

In 1987, the Office of Cooperative Education, in cooperation with Howard University, initiated the Historically Black Colleges and Universities Project through a grant from the U.S. Department of Education. The purpose of this project was to promote cooperative education programs at HPBCUs either by improving existing programs or by helping to start new ones. As part of this project, staff in the University's co-op office developed a training module called "Co-op Contract for Success" consisting of printed material, a video tape, and computer software. The package, designed for co-op administrators, students, or anyone seeking employment, covered topics such as the interview process and what to expect once a job was acquired. It also contained a computerized listing of college majors and companies with potential jobs in those fields.

In 1987, NUCEA awarded the Southeastern Training Center the Irene G. Bagge Award for creative programming for its work with the HPBCU project and conference.

1985

SAFE STATE BEGINS A HAZARDOUS MATERIALS/WASTE MANAGEMENT ASSISTANCE PROGRAM.

CCS

THE HISTORICALLY AND PREDOMINANTLY BLACK COLLEGES AND UNIVERSITIES (HPBCU) PROJECT PROVIDES VALUABLE ASSISTANCE TO ESTABLISHED AND BEGINNING COOPERATIVE EDUCATION PROGRAMS AT HPBCUs ACROSS THE NATION.

In addition to the HPBCU conference, the Southeastern Training Center for Cooperative Education mounted conferences in a number of locations regionally to provide training for supervisors, managers, human resource personnel, and anyone working with co-op students. These conferences served federal agencies and private companies employing co-op students, as well as other colleges and universities' cooperative education programs. In 1983, the Southeastern Training Center initiated a federal government co-op conference which draws 200–400 participants annually.

Independent Study Division

The Independent Study Division entered a new and important period during this time. As part of the systems development plan Dr. Prisk implemented for the College, the Independent Study Division automated its operations using the College's IBM System 36. Registrations, records of lessons received and graded, payroll for teachers, and other functions previously handled manually were now handled by computer. This innovation not only saved time and was more efficient, but also meant that Independent Study staff could quickly access subsets of students by geographic region, courses taken, and other fields as a means of learning more about the profile of the correspondence study student.

In 1987, a new director was appointed after Dr. Nancy Williams retired. Dr. Williams had served as Director of Independent Study for 13 years and had worked in other capacities for the College prior to that.

Enrollments, which declined by close to 10 percent in 1984–85, began a gradual climb for 1985–86 and 1986–87 so that by 1987 the Division was having the best year of the 1980s with 2,449 enrollments (1,261 in college courses and 1,188 in high school courses).

As had been the case when Independent Study first began early in the Extension Division's history, the goals and objectives of the Division continued to be vital to The University of Alabama's mission to extend academic resources to non-traditional students to refresh, update, and/or redirect them.

Law Enforcement Academy

From 1983–88, the Law Enforcement Academy maintained five basic training sessions per year and showed significant increases in enrollments in the Advanced Programs. In addition, it pioneered the Reserve/Auxiliary Law Enforcement Training Programs for the state and was the only academy in the state to offer this training on a continuous basis. Also, the Academy conducted numerous special training seminars for

---

1985

U.S. JUSTICE DEPARTMENT SELECTS THE LAW ENFORCEMENT ACADEMY AS MODEL ACADEMY IN THE STATE FOR ITS AGILITY AND FIREARMS TRAINING COURSES.

---

the law enforcement community including an AIDS seminar for first-response personnel.

In 1985, as the result of several lawsuits with the Alabama Corrections Academy based on sex and racial discrimination in training course practices, the U.S. Department of Justice visited all of the law enforcement academies in the state. After these visits, the Department of Justice recognized The University of Alabama's Law Enforcement Academy as the statewide model in the area of agility and firearms training courses, noting that these courses were administered in a non-discriminatory manner. Further, it mandated that guidelines from the University's academy should be adopted by all other academies in the state because they met Alabama Peace Officer and Standards Training Commissions guidelines and were not discriminatory in any manner.

The Academy showed statewide leadership in other areas as well. Captain Russell Summerlin, the director, was asked to serve as interim acting director for the Northeast Police Academy at Jacksonville State University in 1988 and worked closely with the commission and president of Jacksonville State University in this endeavor. Captain Summerlin also served for 11 consecutive years, from 1972–83, as president of the Alabama Academy Directors Association. During this time the Academy was the southeastern representative and one of three regional police firearm instructor training schools with the National Rifle Association.

The Bryant Conference Center

President Thomas had announced that the Bryant Conference Center complex project was underway in 1983. By 1985, all hurdles had been cleared and the ground-breaking for the complex was held on November 20 of that year.

University officials, city of Tuscaloosa dignitaries, and friends and family of the late Coach Paul "Bear" Bryant assembled for the site dedication under the trees just north of

TUSCALOOSA MAYOR AL DUPONT, CONTINUING STUDIES DEAN DENNIS PRISK, HOTEL DEVELOPER FRANK NIX, BRYANT MUSEUM COMMITTEE MEMBER YOUNG BOOZER, COACH RAY PERKINS, ALUMNI AFFAIRS DIRECTOR ROBERT KIRKSEY, AND UA PRESIDENT JOAB L. THOMAS VIEWED THE ARCHITECT'S MODEL OF THE BRYANT COMPLEX AT THE SITE DEDICATION.

the main campus, directly across Bryant Drive from Memorial (later Coleman) Coliseum. Addressing the group, Dr. Thomas announced that the complex, which included the Sheraton Capstone Inn, Paul W. Bryant Conference Center, Alumni Hall, and Paul W. Bryant Museum, was expected to be open by December 1987, with the Sheraton probably opening first, in late 1986. He said that the Center would help the University bolster its academic and outreach programs and contribute to the development of Tuscaloosa County.

Showing an architect's model of the complex, Dr. Thomas pointed out that the designers, the architectural firms of Giattina-Kirkwood-Fisher of Birmingham and Skidmore-

---

1985

FIRST ANNUAL HISTORICALLY BLACK COLLEGES AND UNIVERSITIES COOPERATIVE EDUCATION CONFERENCE HELD IN WINSTON-SALEM, NC; SPONSORED BY A GRANT FROM THE U.S. DEPARTMENT OF EDUCATION.

Owings-Merrill of Boston, had set out to evoke the features of the University's historic central campus. Pedestrian walkways would connect the four buildings on a 12-acre site, creating a mall with the Bryant Museum in the center.

Local officials commented that the University's expansion would stimulate the local economy, and Dr. Prisk noted that the Bryant Conference Center would attract people with corporate power and influence to the University campus, thus creating opportunities for Tuscaloosa to promote itself as a good place for living and investing.

By December 1986, the $10-million Sheraton Capstone Inn opened for business, although it did not hold its public ribbon- cutting ceremony until February 1987. Private investors with strong ties to the University built and managed the hotel which had 150 stylish hotel rooms, including executive and king suites. The hotel was available to house conferees and cater functions at the Bryant Conference Center, as well as serve the University and Tuscaloosa communities' lodging and catered function needs. A restaurant and upscale lounge rounded out the hotel's features.

On October 30, 1987, the 64,000-square-foot Bryant Conference Center was officially dedicated and open for business two months ahead of schedule. The opening of the facility marked the realization of a dream for continuing education professionals on campus. For the first time in the history of extension and continuing education at The University of Alabama, a facility second-to-none was available for the education of those outside traditional enrollment strategies. To ensure the Bryant Conference Center's attractiveness to conference planners, all media technologies selected were the best available, designed to enhance and enrich the teaching-learning process. The Center would touch the lives of many people,

---

1985

Ground-breaking ceremonies for the Bryant Conference Center, Sheraton Capstone Inn, Alumni Hall, and Bryant Museum held in November.

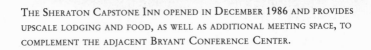

THE SHERATON CAPSTONE INN OPENED IN DECEMBER 1986 AND PROVIDES
UPSCALE LODGING AND FOOD, AS WELL AS ADDITIONAL MEETING SPACE, TO
COMPLEMENT THE ADJACENT BRYANT CONFERENCE CENTER.

as well as pay tribute to the memory of the late Coach Paul W.
Bryant.

At the opening night ceremonies, Dr. Thomas hosted a
reception and dinner for the fall meeting of his advisory
cabinet. Addressing his cabinet, Dr. Thomas said that "continuing education is a growth area and the Bryant Conference
Center will help the University of Alabama remain on the
leading edge of the trend."

As a means of demonstrating the media technology of the
Center, Dr. Prisk and center director Dr. Robert W. Hudson

1985

ENRICHING THE ADULT STUDENT ENVIRONMENT (EASE), A SUPPORT GROUP FOR
ADULT STUDENTS, BEGINS REGULAR WEEKLY MEETINGS IN MARTHA PARHAM WEST.

CCS

A MEDIA CENTER AT THE HEART OF THE BRYANT CONFERENCE CENTER ON THE
SECOND FLOOR HOUSES ALL EQUIPMENT, INCLUDING THE VIDEO RECORDING AND
EDITING SYSTEM, AND SERVES AS A BASE OF OPERATION FOR MEDIA TECHNICIANS.

arranged for a presentation of video-taped remarks from two
dignitaries who could not attend the ceremony in person.
Alabama governor Guy Hunt and Mr. Ichiro Shinji, chairman,
Victor Company of Japan (JVC) both offered congratulatory
remarks via videotape.

Dr. Prisk narrated a demonstration of the Bryant Conference Center's sound, video, and audio-visual capabilities. He
noted that the Center's communication and information systems had been carefully designed to facilitate continuing education programs. These technologies, together with the

1986
FIRST ANNUAL RETURNING ADULT STUDENT SEMINAR HELD PRIOR TO FALL SEMESTER
TO ORIENT ADULT STUDENTS TO SERVICES AND PROGRAMS AT THE UNIVERSITY.

Alumni Hall, adjacent to the Bryant Complex, opened in 1987.

Center's trained media technicians, would provide a richly enhanced learning environment.

In addition to the basic inventory of audio-visual equipment, the Bryant Conference Center featured a closed-circuit television system, a video recording and editing system, teleconferencing capabilities, an audio recording system, video projectors, an auditorium with a centralized-control podium system and a projector system, and a telephone intercom system.

Also dedicated the same evening as the Center was the Alumni Hall, adjacent to the Bryant Conference Center. National Alumni Association President Walt Graham said that the association would move into its new headquarters before the end of the year, after 40 years in its present building.

Some of the first conferences scheduled to be held in the new center during 1987–88, its first year of operation, included: the Metal Casting Technology Center's Second

---

1986

The Sheraton Capstone Inn first to open within the four-building complex containing the Bryant Conference Center, Bryant Museum, and Alumni Hall.

UNIVERSITY RELATIONS

THE BRYANT CONFERENCE CENTER OPENED IN OCTOBER 1987. MR. WILLIAM
D. SELLERS, JR., ONE OF THE CENTER'S BENEFACTORS, CUT THE RIBBON IN
FRONT OF THE SELLERS AUDITORIUM. (L-R) BRYANT CENTER EXECUTIVE
DIRECTOR DR. ROBERT HUDSON, UA PRESIDENT DR. JOAB THOMAS, AND
CONTINUING STUDIES DEAN DR. DENNIS P. PRISK PROUDLY ASSIST.

Annual Industry Symposium, Legal Aspects of Death and
Dying, the Coalbed Methane Conference, the statewide 41st
Annual Federal Tax Clinic, and a training conference for
Mutual of New York (MONY).

From its first full year of operation, 1988–89, the Center
hosted approximately 350 programs, representing 30,000 attendees. The opening of the Bryant Conference Center, perhaps more than any single event in the history of extension
and continuing education at the University, represented a

1986

SAFE STATE BECOMES THE ALABAMA DESIGNEE FOR TRAINING AND CERTIFICATION OF
ASBESTOS ABATEMENT PERSONNEL UNDER U.S. ENVIRONMENTAL PROTECTION
AGENCY REGULATIONS.

THE PAUL W. BRYANT MUSEUM OPENED OCTOBER 8, 1988,
COMPLETING THE $20-MILLION BRYANT COMPLEX. CELEBRITIES AND
UNIVERSITY SUPPORTERS GATHERED FOR THE EVENT.

ALABAMA MUSEUMS DIRECTOR DR. DOUGLAS JONES, PAUL W. BRYANT, JR., AND
(L–R) JOHN DAVID CROWE, JR. VIEW THE HEISMAN TROPHY WON BY CROWE'S
FATHER IN 1957. THE CROWE FAMILY DONATED THE TROPHY TO THE MUSEUM.

AT THE MUSEUM OPENING, (L-R) FORMER BRYANT PLAYER VAUGHN MANCHA,
BIRMINGHAM POST HERALD SPORTSWRITER BILL LUMPKIN, AND SPORTS
BROADCASTER MEL ALLEN REMINISCED ABOUT COACH BRYANT.

dramatic widening of the circle of adult learners on and off the UA campus. People would travel to the Bryant Conference Center from across the state, the nation, and around the world to learn and to share their knowledge in the continuing education process. A number of historic conferences took place in the Center during its first few years of operation, including the "Opening Doors: An Appraisal of Race Relations in America" conference in June 1988 which commemorated the 25th anniversary of the integration of The University of Alabama.

Remodeling of Martha Parham West

From 1983 until 1988, Martha Parham West, which had served as the continuing education center for many years, underwent a number of renovations. These included relocating the reception area to the main lobby and remodeling it, relocating and consolidating the suite of offices for the dean's staff, and relocating the Law Enforcement Academy from Martha Parham East to Martha Parham West. Also, rooms J and K, which had previously served as meeting rooms were remodeled as offices for the Safe State staff and the kitchen area was designated as the Safe State laboratory.

On the second and third floors of the building, rooms were carpeted and painted; offices and divisions were assigned contiguous space. The fourth floor was painted and carpeted and designated for the International Trade Center (not a part of the College) and for the Division of Environmental and Industrial Program's administrative offices. The fifth floor, also painted and carpeted, housed the Law School Clinical Programs.

1986-87

DIVISION OF ENVIRONMENTAL AND INDUSTRIAL PROGRAMS (DEIP) IS FORMED BY COMBINING CONTINUING ENGINEERING EDUCATION, OSHA TRAINING PROGRAMS, AND SAFE STATE.

Room M, also previously a large open meeting area, was remodeled beginning in spring 1988 to accommodate Cooperative Education which would be moving to the building from Comer Hall across campus. Room B was outfitted appropriately to serve as the computer lab for professional development computer training courses.

Thus, as the Bryant Conference Center became a reality, all of the program and administrative units of the College were now housed in updated offices, located conveniently near each other for maximum efficiency.

Goals for the 1990s

By 1988, the College of Continuing Studies administration and staff had addressed the major goals set forward by Dr. Prisk. The major reorganization of the College was in place, extensive program development had been accomplished and was still growing, the Bryant Complex was open and functioning, and the College's offices and systems were fully automated. Growth of the College in many ways had been accelerated during the five years from 1983–88, with a doubling of program offerings. At this point, in a summary report of the past five years, Dr. Prisk articulated challenges facing the College.

He noted that the College of Continuing Studies is an organization capable of serving as a force for experimenting with risk venture in a controlled and organized manner. The College would continue to operate in partnership with other colleges/schools within the University. In some instances, the College would be prepared to move on its own to design and implement programs. As the College looked to the future, Dr. Prisk felt the following would be of importance:

* continue to strengthen the College's relationship with other colleges and schools within the University

1987

BRYANT CONFERENCE CENTER AND ALUMNI HALL OPEN.

* continue to emphasize professional updating programs
* establish an interdisciplinary undergraduate degree
* increase emphasis on technology to enhance the learning process
* increase risk capital for new program initiatives
* seek more collaborative relationships with other providers of continuing education
* increase emphasis on developing the applied research capabilities of the College
* refine the market research capabilities of the College
* develop more financial assistance for adult students
* continue to diversify the College's fiscal base

In his report, Dr. Prisk wrote, "The College of Continuing Studies is poised to remain a prominent force in meeting the needs of older students. As it continues to refine its capabilities, and with continued institutional support, the College represents a system for adaptation and change that will make The University of Alabama a leader in continuing education."

Dr. Prisk had realized, through program development and construction of the Bryant Conference Center, many of the dreams articulated in the early 1970s by Dr. Drewry. Further, the College's evolution as a major provider of continuing education in the state coincided with the visions of all the deans of extension and continuing education who had come before him: that The University of Alabama should be a leader in the field of adult and continuing education in the state, the region, and even the nation.

Dr. Prisk remained at the University until mid-1989, when he left to take a post as assistant vice-president for Extended Education at Arizona State University in Tempe, Arizona. Shortly before, associate dean Dr. Robert B. Leiter had re-

1987
COOPERATIVE EDUCATION INITIATES THE HISTORICALLY BLACK COLLEGES AND UNIVERSITIES PROJECT THROUGH A GRANT FROM THE U.S. DEPARTMENT OF EDUCATION.

signed to become dean of Continuing Education at Mississippi State University.

For his last year as dean, Dr. Prisk counted among the highlights for the College the completed renovation of Martha Parham West, and the first full year of operation for the Bryant Conference Center. The center had exceeded all expectations in terms of attendance, number of programs, and income. Also, the College had continued to achieve success in the area of private giving. As it had continued to do for the previous four years, the College's income and programs had grown significantly. Dr. Prisk noted that from 1983 to mid-1989, the College's income had increased by 36 percent. "From the perspective of facilities, staff, organizational structure, quality and diversity of programs, income, and campus relations, the College is in excellent shape," he wrote.

University Relations

Dr. E. Roger Sayers

Dr. E. Roger Sayers Named
University President, 1989

Dr. Thomas resigned as president of the University in August 1988. Dr. E. Roger Sayers, formerly vice-president for

---

1988

Paul W. Bryant Museum opens adjacent to the Bryant Conference Center and Sheraton Capstone Inn.

---

academic affairs, was named acting president of the University and was confirmed as president in July 1989. Like Dr. Thomas, Dr. Sayers would maintain a strong commitment to continuing education at The University of Alabama.

DR. ROBERT W. HUDSON

Interim, 1989–90

Dr. Robert W. Hudson, director of the Bryant Conference Center, served as interim dean of the College of Continuing Studies from September 1989 through July 1990.

During the year that Dr. Hudson served as interim dean for the College, on-going programs continued to thrive and growth continued to be excellent.

Services to the adult student continued through such programs as the Returning Adult Student Seminar and the EASE (Enriching the Adult Student Environment) program. In ad-

---

1989

DR. E. ROGER SAYERS, FORMERLY VICE-PRESIDENT FOR ACADEMIC AFFAIRS, NAMED PRESIDENT OF THE UNIVERSITY OF ALABAMA.

---

dition to the adult student and incarcerated persons scholarships already in place, the recently endowed Clarice L. Parker Memorial Scholarship was awarded for the first time.

The Cooperative Education Program continued to expand and in this year had an enrollment of approximately 350 co-op students. Other activities within the co-op office included the administration of a number of conference and workshops in the region by the Southeastern Training Center for Cooperative Education, and the expansion of co-op programs at HPBCUs.

In other programming areas, Dr. Hudson noted the following highlights in his 1989–90 Annual Report and Institutional Plan:

* The Safe State/Toxic Substance Control Program continued as the Governor's designee for training and accreditation of asbestos abatement personnel under U. S. Environmental Protection Agency regulations and the Alabama Asbestos Contractor Accreditation Act. In addition, Safe State was the Governor's designee to review and approve asbestos management and abatement plans and actions proposed by Alabama's public/private primary and secondary schools.
* The Division of Environmental and Industrial programs was again supported by more than $1.5 million in external funding.
* The Gadsden Educational Center continued to show steady growth with a 23 percent increase in enrollment and an 11 percent increase in course offerings. During this time, Gadsden initiated the "A" Master's Degree in Special Education with concentrations in mild learning handicapped (MLH), learning disabled (LD), and emotional conflict (EC).

1989

DR. ROBERT W. HUDSON, DIRECTOR OF THE BRYANT CONFERENCE CENTER AND HOTEL, NAMED INTERIM DEAN OF CONTINUING STUDIES; SERVES UNTIL JULY 1990.

---

* The Child Development Associate Training Program had 146 candidates from 22 Alabama counties enrolled, and signed and implemented 13 Memoranda of Agreement for training preschool staff.
* The Division of Instructional Programs increased total enrollments by 19.5 percent. This represented a sixth consecutive year of growth, a trend expected to continue in 1990–91.
* The Law Enforcement Academy inaugurated a one-of-a-kind Jail Management Program for the state of Alabama.
* Expanded efficiency in use of the College's Macintosh computer system and the Linotronic output services of University Printing and Duplicating increased the College's marketing production capabilities and creativity.
* Use of the Bryant Conference Center continued to grow and was ahead of schedule in terms of projected revenues and 5-year pro forma goals.
* All sales and marketing efforts for the Bryant Conference Center and Sheraton Capstone Inn were centralized under the title "Bryant Conference Center and Hotel."
* The Division of Professional and Management Development Programs continued its strong growth in both public enrollment courses, contract activities, and new program initiatives.

* * * * *

1983–1990 were important years of evolution for the College of Continuing Studies. A major reorganization of the College together with accelerated program growth and the acquisition of long-sought-for facilities and technologies had enabled the College to come of age on The University of Alabama campus. The College had become, beyond question, the state leader in continuing education. The stage was now set for regional and national leadership.

1989

DR. PHILIP E. AUSTIN IS NAMED CHANCELLOR OF THE UNIVERSITY OF ALABAMA SYSTEM.

CHAPTER 8

THE TECHNOLOGICAL CHALLENGE

Era of Dr. John C. Snider, 1990–present

Approaching the dawn of the twenty-first century, the College of Continuing Studies found itself advantageously poised for the future. Able to reach many more people through a greater variety of program offerings and state-of-the-art facilities and technology, Continuing Studies had never been in a better position to extend the services of The University of Alabama than it was in 1990.

In the summer of 1990, Dr. John C. Snider, former secretary for the State Board of Agriculture and vice chancellor of academic affairs for the Colorado State University System, was named dean of the College of Continuing Studies. Upon his arrival in August, Dr. Snider found a highly diverse continuing education unit offering a variety of credit and noncredit programs, as well as other services such as health and safety consultation, law enforcement training, and cooperative education.

Addressing the College staff at the annual meeting in October of that year, Dr. Snider expressed his ambitious vision for the growth of the College. "It is my hope," he said, "that the University of Alabama College of Continuing Studies will become one of the leading continuing education units in the nation by 1995, and recognized as such by sister institutions

CROSBY THOMLEY

"IT IS MY HOPE THAT THE UNIVERSITY OF ALABAMA COLLEGE OF CONTINUING STUDIES WILL BECOME ONE OF THE LEADING CONTINU- ING EDUCATION UNITS IN THE NATION BY 1995, AND RECOGNIZED AS SUCH BY SISTER INSTITU- TIONS."

DR. JOHN C. SNIDER

such as those representative of NUCEA and ACHE member- ship. In other words, we must grow from number-one status in Alabama to top ranking at the national level."

In assessing the College's potential to be recognized as a national leader in continuing education, Dr. Snider formu- lated long-range goals for the College. He announced these to the staff in the October 1990 meeting. Some of the goals were major in scope and would require funding, extra assignments for staff, and major equipment outlays, but none of the goals Dr. Snider outlined was beyond the capabilities of the College as it was currently organized.

His five-year goals were ambitious:

* By 1995, the Bryant Conference Center and Hotel would conduct more than 700 conferences annually.
* The Division of Professional and Management Develop- ment Programs (PMDP) would initiate and head a nationwide consortium of colleges and universities in

1990

DR. JOHN C. SNIDER NAMED DEAN OF COLLEGE OF CONTINUING STUDIES.

order to efficiently and effectively offer nationally competitive, cutting-edge professional development programs.

* The Division of PMDP would greatly expand its computer-assisted laboratory programs utilizing a new, sophisticated lab to be placed in the Cahaba Room of Martha Parham West.
* The Division of PMDP would explore the potential for a working relationship with the leadership of the expanded Birmingham Civic Center in order to enhance its professional development programming.
* The Division of Independent Study would greatly increase its course offerings and reach an annual enrollment level of 6,000 by 1995.
* The Law Enforcement Academy would not only increase enrollments in the basic program but also increase its advanced-level courses and seminars by 200 percent, including computer-assisted programs.
* The Division of Environmental and Industrial Programs would expand the scope of Safe State and triple the number of DEIP executive- and advanced-level programs with greater emphasis on nationally targeted markets.
* Cooperative Education would expand its base by significantly increasing the number of University students participating in the program and by offering additional advanced training programs nationally.
* The Division of Instructional Programs would expand its enrollments by 35 percent and deliver 3 to 5 new graduate degree programs off campus, primarily in the Montgomery, Gadsden, and Dothan communities. In addition, the Division would implement a complete and successful "evening program" in the Tuscaloosa/West Alabama region. This would constitute a major new programming thrust for the College.
* The College and the Dean's office would research, de-

velop, and implement a new unit of the College for telecommunications. This new unit would deliver its first courses via television by the fall 1991 semester. The program would primarily consist of credit courses offered for graduate and undergraduate credit. The courses would be delivered both in-state and nationally. Complete master's degree programs would be delivered by 1995.

Dr. Snider asked Reggie Smith, director of the Division of Instructional Programs, to head the evening programs initiative, as it logically fell within his area.

"Telecommunication," Dr. Snider said, "will need to rise from dreams." He announced that three current staff members would assist him in the creation of the program. Carroll Tingle, director of the Adult Student Office, was named acting director of the office; David Musick, head media technician at the Bryant Conference Center and Hotel, would oversee technical responsibilities, and JoAnn Devereaux, from the Office of College Relations, was tapped to oversee off-campus relations with business and industry—the primary clients of the program.

Foreseeing a bright but challenging future, Dr. Snider encouraged the staff to work together. "It will take creative marketing, solid budgeting, outstanding public relations, and client-centered advising to realize our goals," he said. "Whether in programming or support services, we all must function as a team."

From the time Dr. Snider made these announcements until he met with the College staff again in the fall of 1991, significant progress was made toward the goals.

Educational Telecommunications

Dr. Snider turned his attention quickly to the goal of establishing the Office of Educational Telecommunications, first housed within the Adult Student Office, and later made a freestanding division within the College. Carroll Tingle was named director.

"Telecommunications," a broad term involving a variety of delivery systems, refers to the use of videotape to record and duplicate classes; interactive, live video transmissions that link a number of classrooms during the period of instruction; fiber optics; satellite up- and down-linking; and other technologically enhanced methods of instruction. It was Dr. Snider's intention to move The University of Alabama College of Continuing Studies forward in the area of telecommunications, which, by 1991, had become an increasingly popular, and necessary, delivery method for academic programs around the country.

In the spring of 1991, Dr. Snider and the staff of Educational Telecommunications began working with other colleges on campus to initiate a selection of video-based undergraduate and graduate courses. The program was named QUEST, an acronym for Quality University Extended Site Telecourses, and was modeled on the SURGE telecommunications program with which Dr. Snider had worked previously at Colorado State University. The QUEST program offered its first slate of courses in fall 1991 in nursing, business, engineering, and library and information studies.

A classroom in the College of Engineering's East Engineering

1991

The Office of Educational Telecommunications is created. The QUEST (Quality University Extended Site Telecourses) program is initiated as well as the IITS (Intercampus Interactive Telecommunications System) for simultaneously-linked classes and meetings for the three campuses of The University of Alabama System.

GRADUATE AND UNDERGRADUATE COURSES IN THE QUEST CLASSROOM ARE
VIDEOTAPED FOR NEXT DAY SHIPMENT TO QUEST SITES THROUGHOUT ALABAMA
WHERE WORKING ADULTS AND OTHERS CAN PURSUE DEGREES WITHOUT LEAVING
THEIR JOBS OR DISRUPTING THEIR LIVES. HERE, COLLEGE OF ENGINEERING DEAN
BOB BARFIELD AND QUEST DIRECTOR CARROLL TINGLE TEST VIDEOTAPE.

building was completely renovated and equipped as the
QUEST classroom, with the College of Engineering and the
College of Continuing Studies sharing expenses. Video cam-
eras, microphones, two large color monitors, and a media
center at the back of the room were installed and make it
possible for classes to be videotaped and mailed to QUEST
sites the following day. At these QUEST sites around the state
of Alabama, students can view the tapes and progress through
the course with their on-campus "classmates." Professors are
available for office hours via telephone. Exams are sent to the
sites and proctored by approved site coordinators.

With the QUEST system in place, The University of Ala-

THE INTERCAMPUS INTERACTIVE TELECOMMUNICATIONS SYSTEM (IITS) CONSISTS OF TECHNOLOGICALLY EQUIPPED CLASSROOMS ON THE THREE CAMPUSES OF THE UNIVERSITY OF ALABAMA SYSTEM LINKED FOR SIMULTANEOUS, INTERACTIVE CLASSES OR MEETINGS.

bama now has the potential to provide off-campus courses by video-based instruction virtually anywhere, providing that a site has been established. Sites generally are setup within a corporate or other workplace setting, a public library, or similar public place. As the QUEST program grew from 1991-92, sites were established at a number of locations around Alabama, Georgia, and Mississippi. QUEST thus enables working professionals to continue their education and stay current in their fields without leaving their jobs or disrupting their lives.

Another telecommunications effort, the Intercampus Interactive Telecommunications System (IITS), also started in fall 1991 in an effort to share the expertise of the three campuses of The University of Alabama System through interactive video. Housed in the Cahaba Room of Martha Parham West, the IITS program facilitates live, interactive video classrooms and meetings. For instance, as a professor teaches a course in public relations to students in the IITS classroom on the Tuscaloosa campus, students in classrooms at The University of Alabama in Huntsville and at The University of Alabama in Birmingham can simultaneously view the professor and students in Tuscaloosa on monitors. With the aid of interactive equipment at UAH and UAB, the professor in Tuscaloosa can answer questions of students at the other locations. Thus the classroom is truly extended, simultaneously, without the professor's ever having left his or her campus. The IITS link provides the capability for courses to originate from Huntsville and Birmingham also. By combining the talents of educators in The University of Alabama System with the interactive telecommunications resources, IITS expands educational opportunities statewide and contributes to building a university system for the telecommunications age.

In addition to QUEST and IITS, the office of Educational Telecommunications began to develop, market, and administer video short courses from various disciplines. Courses in computer science and management were taped and marketed during 1991–92. Future plans include further course development for QUEST, establishment of additional sites, connecting IITS to other locations with compatible interactive video equipment, and satellite delivery.

The overall mission of the Office of Educational Telecommunications is to make quality, up-to-date education available in a flexible, convenient manner, extending the resources of the University to all citizens of the state of Alabama. Potential for expansion of this program is virtually limitless as all areas of The University of Alabama come to understand the possibilities for extending the institution's resources through telecommunications.

1991

UNI-LINK CONSORTIUM OF CONTINUING EDUCATION UNITS FROM 15 UNIVERSITIES ACROSS THE COUNTRY IS LAUNCHED, UNDER THE AUSPICES OF THE DIVISION OF PROFESSIONAL AND MANAGEMENT DEVELOPMENT PROGRAMS.

Uni-Link Consortium Sets National Standard

Another of Dr. Snider's major goals for the College was the development of a national consortium of universities' professional development programs. Beginning in 1990, this initiative was spearheaded by the College's Division of Professional and Management Development Programs under the direction of Tom Wingenter, who had originally proposed the national consortium concept. Termed "Uni-Link," this innovative concept was conceived as a way to serve businesses and organizations seeking top results from noncredit training and professional development.

The consortium is made up of 15 leading universities. Each is committed to extending to a national market premium short courses and certificate programs. Only those programs with proven track records are offered to Uni-Link by member universities. Member institutions opt to participate in any given offering based on the topic and their individual situations. The emphasis is on quality, accessibility, cost effectiveness, and ultimately, profitability.

By 1992, Uni-Link's membership consisted of universities from all parts of the United States, including UCLA, Colorado State University, University of Miami, and University of Wisconsin-Milwaukee. Administratively anchored at The University of Alabama College of Continuing Studies, Uni-Link's member institutions coordinate their offerings, calendars, marketing, and service delivery with one another through the College. From a national perspective, this means a greater variety of top-flight, competitively priced noncredit courses are available. The concept of offering each member institution's "star" noncredit resources to a national market fulfills Dr. Snider's desire that the University of Alabama College of Continuing Studies take the lead nationally in the area of professional development continuing education. In Uni-Link, the sum has potential for being greater than the parts.

Reorganization Prefigures University Downsizing

In June 1991, Dr. Snider announced several changes in the College's organization that, in effect, prefigured the downsizing that the University would soon begin to undertake as a result of proration and budget constraints.

Three divisions were disbanded and their professional and clerical staff incorporated into other divisions. The Office of College Relations was dissolved and its director, Ed Conyers, made special assistant to the dean, continuing his fund-raising and public relations activities. The Adult Student Office was merged with the Division of Instructional Programs, with Marius Jones, formerly from Cooperative Education, being named assistant director. Carroll Tingle, former ASO director, was made director of the new Office of Educational Telecommunications.

The other major reorganizational change consisted of disbanding the Office of Marketing and Communications, thus decentralizing the marketing function, and expanding the Office of Budget and Planning under the direction of Duane Cunningham to include mailing list coordination and graphic arts with the new name Office of Administrative Services. Other marketing professionals and support staff were relocated in programming divisions. To keep the College up to date on marketing issues relating to direct mail, quantity discounts, and other aspects of promotion, a Marketing Council was established and charged to meet regularly and report to appropriate directors and Dr. Snider. With further budget cuts and additional proration expected in the coming year, streamlining the College's divisions added efficiency without the detrimental effect of losing staff or programs.

1991

ADULT STUDENT OFFICE MERGES WITH THE DIVISION OF INSTRUCTIONAL PROGRAMS.

THE UNIVERSITY OF ALABAMA
COLLEGE OF CONTINUING STUDIES

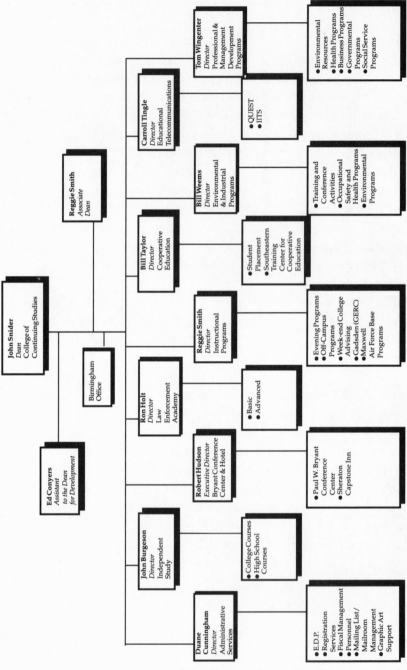

September 1, 1992

IN 1991 THE COLLEGE OF CONTINUING STUDIES WAS REORGANIZED TO EMPHASIZE PROGRAMMING UNITS, WITH ALL ADMINISTRATIVE AND GRAPHIC ARTS SUPPORT SERVICES BEING CONTAINED IN ONE OFFICE.

CCS

THE NEW UA EVENING PROGRAM BEGAN IN FALL 1991 UNDER THE AUSPICES OF THE COLLEGE OF CONTINUING STUDIES.

Evening Program

By fall 1991, the College was ready to offer, through the Division of Instructional Programs, its slate of courses grouped under the heading Evening Program. The program would allow adults to attend classes at night in order to complete degrees while maintaining family or job responsibilities. The schedule contained more than 60 courses. Both the bachelor's degree in management and the master's degree in human resources management were scheduled as major emphases of the new program. Seen as a way to fulfill the needs of working adults unable to attend classes during daytime, or business hours, Evening Program, under the direction of Reggie Smith, made it possible for more people to work toward degrees at night.

1991

REORGANIZATION OF THE COLLEGE RESULTS IN FORMATION OF OFFICE OF ADMINIS-TRATIVE SERVICES, WHICH INCLUDES BUDGET AND PLANNING, REGISTRATION SERVICES, GRAPHICS DEPARTMENT, AND MAILING LIST SERVICES FOR THE COLLEGE.

Evening Program was heavily marketed in the West Alabama area for the fall 1991 and spring 1992 semesters, and in summer 1992. By fall 1992, Evening Program had 70 courses in its catalog. During the first year of operation the program had enrolled more than 800 students. Close to 900 students were expected to enroll through the Evening Program in fall 1992, with most academic colleges represented by that time. Evening Program was the first major step in Dr. Snider's plan to facilitate working adults' efforts to attain undergraduate and graduate degrees after working hours from the University. For many people for whom daytime classes are not an option, Evening Program, under the direction of Reggie Smith, now promises an avenue toward advanced education and career growth.

College Opens Birmingham Civic Center Office

On April 1, 1991, the College opened a Birmingham office in the expanded Birmingham Jefferson Civic Center on behalf of The University of Alabama. Under a three-year lease agreement with the Civic Center, the office consists of a classroom and an office staffed by one full-time support person. Other space is available for rental as needed from the Civic Center for conference activities too extensive to be handled by the Bryant Conference Center and Hotel or other facilities in Tuscaloosa.

The Civic Center office facilitates a number of The University of Alabama's continuing education activities already in place in the Birmingham area, such as Weekend College

---

1990-91

COOPERATIVE EDUCATION DIVISION BEGINS A GRADUATE CO-OP PROGRAM IN COOPERATION WITH THE GRADUATE SCHOOL OF LIBRARY AND INFORMATION SERVICE. DURING THIS TIME, CO-OP PLACEMENTS REACH AN ALL-TIME HIGH OF 352 STUDENTS PLACED IN JOBS RELATED TO THEIR COLLEGE MAJORS.

---

courses and courses offered through Instructional Programs toward the master's degree program in library and information service. Noncredit offerings that appeal to national or international audiences held at the Civic Center will benefit from proximity to the Birmingham airport. And noncredit courses heavily targeted to constituencies in the Birmingham area will benefit from the office and classroom. The Civic Center office is also a designated QUEST site. The first program held at the new office in August 1992 was a three-day personal-effectiveness seminar managed by the Division of Professional and Management Development Programs and directed toward engineering and technically-oriented professionals.

1991 Summary of Accomplishments

Reporting to the Office of Academic Affairs in June 1991, Dr. Snider summarized the accomplishments of the College, noting that "in spite of serious financial constraints, the College completed a rather successful year that included a broad range of program activities that have provided continuing education opportunities to approximately 55,000 adult, part-time students.

"It is the expectation of the entire CCS staff," Dr. Snider wrote, "that growth will continue in 1991–92 and that the College of Continuing Studies will continue to serve the lifelong learning needs of the people of Alabama and the nation."

At the annual College meeting in fall 1991, Dr. Snider reiterated this point, reminding those assembled that as a college, Continuing Studies had contributed its "fair share to proration" during the past fiscal year, that there had been no salary increases for 1991–92, and that additional proration in the University budget was imminent. However, Dr. Snider said that he was very proud of the College's accomplishments,

THE DIVISION OF INSTRUCTIONAL PROGRAMS OFFERS A MASTER'S DEGREE IN
MILITARY HISTORY AND A DOCTORATE OF PUBLIC ADMINISTRATION IN
MONTGOMERY AT MAXWELL AIR FORCE BASE. DEGREES ARE CONFERRED
IN A COMPLETE GRADUATION CEREMONY HELD ON BASE EACH MAY.

and he asked the division directors to give area highlights,
including current programming initiatives and other accomplishments.

Highlights of the 1990–91 fiscal year, in addition to those
already noted, included:

* The Division of Instructional Programs began the
  Evening Program in fall 1990. The Gadsden Education
  and Research Center enrolled the first students in its new
  master's degree and "class A" certification programs in
  learning disabilities, emotional conflict, and mild learning handicapped. Plans were also finalized to begin a 15-
  semester-hour core of the master of library service de-

1990-91

THE EASE (ENRICHING THE ADULT STUDENT ENVIRONMENT) PROGRAM IS
RECOGNIZED AS AN OFFICIAL CAMPUS ORGANIZATION.

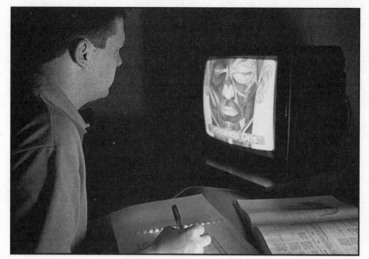

THE INDEPENDENT STUDY DIVISION DEVELOPED FOUR NEW COURSES IN 1990–91
INCORPORATING VIDEO TAPES AS PART OF THE INSTRUCTIONAL PACKAGE.

gree at the Gadsden Center. As of fall 1991, the inventory
of programs at the Gadsden Center included more than
25 complete graduate degree or certification programs.

Student enrollments, credit hours, and generated income in Instructional Programs all increased by more
than 10 percent in 1990–91. (Student enrollment was
4,744; 14,779 semester credit hours were generated.) This
represented the seventh consecutive year of significant
growth, with the trend expected to continue. Of particular note was the doctorate of public administration program, offered by the Division at Maxwell Air Force Base,
in which 91 students were enrolled, making it one of the
five largest D.P.A. programs in the United States.

* The Independent Study Division, under the direction of
John Burgeson, published 12 new editions of college
courses. Four new courses were developed with the
added dimension of video tapes used as a part of the
instructional package. Six new editions of high school

THE SELLERS AUDITORIUM IN THE BRYANT CONFERENCE CENTER CAN
ACCOMMODATE DINNER GROUPS OF AS MANY AS 650 AND CAN SEAT UP TO
1,000 PARTICIPANTS THEATER-STYLE.

courses were also published. In addition, five new
courses were added to the high school curriculum.

Enrollments continued to grow at a steady rate in both
the college and high school program. The college-level
program increased its completions for spring graduation
as well as completions for graduation in the high school
program.

* The Office of Cooperative Education began working
with the Graduate School of Library Service to place
students in 1990–91. Under the direction of Dr. Bill
Taylor, the enrollment of co–op students reached an all-
time high of 352 during the 1990–91 academic year. A
small decline due to the recession appeared during summer 1991. The three-year, federally funded project for
Historically and Predominantly Black Colleges and
Universities was successfully completed in December
1990.

* The Bryant Conference Center and Hotel hosted 600 conferences, workshops, meetings, seminars, and other functions during 1990–91, representing a 56 percent increase from the previous year. Use of the Center came from a program mix in approximately equal proportions from the College of Continuing Studies, the University as a whole, and non-University markets represented by both corporate and association programs.

Although the Center drew primarily from a state and regional market base, several programs drew national and international participation. These included the 1991 Coalbed Methane Symposium, the Fourth Annual Association for the Education of Gifted Underachieving Students, the American Institute of Real Estate Appraisers, the National Collegiate Recreational Sports Association, and Interactive Telecommunications in Higher Education: Implementation and Academic Issues.

The Center also formalized a contingency fund to maintain the facility as a showpiece, state-of-the-art conference center. Replacement of carpet began in 1990–91 and was scheduled to continue in increments until completed.

A unique joint marketing effort between the Sheraton Capstone Inn, a privately held facility, and the Bryant Conference Center, operated by the University, was initiated in 1990, led by the Center's executive director Dr. Robert Hudson. Under this arrangement, certain employees of the University who work at the Center report to a Sheraton-employed director of marketing, who in turn reports to the director of the Center. This highly cooperative arrangement allows the properties to be marketed as one entity: The Bryant Conference Center and Hotel.

1991

Law Enforcement Academy graduates 100th session of basic training.

BRYANT CONFERENCE CENTER AND HOTEL
Organizational Chart

JOINT MARKETING / SALES

OPERATIONS - BCC

EXECUTIVE COMMITTEE
Taaffe - UA   Snider - CCS
Wright - UA   Jackson - SCI
et. al.

COORDINATING COMMITTEE
Snider - CCS   Jackson - SCI
Hudson - BCC   Holler - SCI

PRESIDENT
JACKSON
HOSPITALITY SVC.
Jackson

DEAN
CCS
Snider

EXECUTIVE MANAGER
HOTEL
Holler

EXECUTIVE DIRECTOR
BCC
Hudson

DIRECTOR CATERING
SCI

CATERING MANAGER
SCI

CATERING COORDINATOR
SCI

CATERING MANAGER
SCI

SALES MANAGER
SCI

SALES MANAGER
SCI

DIRECTOR MARKETING
SCI

DIRECTOR SALES
SCI

SCHEDULING COORDINATOR
BCC

CONFERENCE MANAGER
BCC

CONFERENCE MANAGER
BCC

CONFERENCE MANAGER
BCC

STAFF ASSISTANT
BCC

SALES ASSISTANT
SCI

CONFERENCE CONCIERGE
BCC

SECRETARY II
BCC

HEAD MEDIA
BCC

MEDIA TECHIN.
BCC

BUILDING MANAGER
BBC

LEAD CUSTODIAN
BCC

CUSTODIAN
BCC

CUSTODIAN
BCC

CUSTODIAN
BCC

CUSTODIAN
BCC

LEGEND:
BCC - Bryant Conference Center
SCI - Sheraton Capstone Inn
CCS - College of Continuing Studies
UA - University Administration

ORGANIZATIONAL CHART OF THE BCC AND H.

*   The Division of Professional and Management Development Programs (PMDP) researched several program opportunities, including surveys on counselor education, certificate programs, nursing certification programs, and HRM certification review courses. Results from a special nationwide survey on certificate programs were documented in a chapter authored by Dr. Snider, Dr. Francine Marasco and Donna Keene called "Institutional Policies and Procedures: Bridges or Barriers?" for *Perspectives on Educational Certificate Programs*, edited by Holt and Lopos, as part of the New Directions for Adult and Continuing Education series published by Jossey-Bass.

PMDP expanded its offerings through new program endeavors (the First Alabama Governor's Conference on Parenting, the Fourth Annual AEGUS Conference, the 1991 Summer Public Policy Institute, Taguchi Techniques, Cryogenics, Valuation of Oil Gas Properties, and Valuation of Industrial Mineral Resources) as well as through the production of new education materials such as publications, videotapes, and software.

A grant proposal to fund nursing continuing education programs was submitted to the U.S. Department of Health and Human Services. Other fund-raising activities included the establishment of an educational grant from the Kettering Foundation, Dayton, Ohio, to help support the Summer Public Policy Institute at The University of Alabama over a three-year period.

* The Division of Environmental and Industrial Programs, under the direction of Bill Weems, submitted seven proposals representing total revenues of $1,127,153 through the University's Office of Sponsored Programs. Five of

---

1991

Evening Programs initiative begins with fall 1991 semester.

IN CONJUNCTION WITH CENTER FOR COMMUNICATION AND EDUCATIONAL TECHNOLOGY (CCET), THE DIVISION OF ENVIRONMENTAL AND INDUSTRIAL PROGRAMS' SAFE STATE DEVELOPED MEGITS, A COMPUTER-BASED TRAINING SYSTEM WHICH UTILIZES AUDIO, VIDEO, TEXT, AND COMPUTER-GENERATED GRAPHICS SIMULTANEOUSLY TO EXPLAIN TERMS AND CONCEPTS RELATED TO THE HEALTH AND SAFETY PROTECTION OF THE WORKER FOUND IN MATERIAL SAFETY DATA SHEETS. UNDERSTANDING OF THESE TERMS AND CONCEPTS IS REQUIRED UNDER OSHA'S HAZARD COMMUNICATION REGULATIONS.

these proposals were awarded by the U.S. Department of Labor-OSHA and the U.S. Environmental Protection Agency: Safe State/OSHA Onsite Consultation Program, OSHA Consultation Training Support Services, OSHA Consultation Forms Management Support, Material Safety Data Sheet (MSDS)-Electronic Glossary, and Interactive Training System (MEGITS), and the Alabama Asbestos Accreditation Data System.

Both the Safe State program and the USDOL-OSHA Consultation Support Services program continued within DEIP. Other programs DEIP mounted or facilitated included the national Annual OSHA Consultation Conference for project managers and OSHA National Office officials (Tucson, AZ); the Managers' Educational

CCS

Program component covering OSHA's Computerized
Integrated Management System (Williamsburg, VA); and
the national meeting of USDOL-OSHA personnel and
the Association of Occupational Safety and Health Consultation Programs (St. Petersburg, FL).

* During 1990–91, under the direction of Ron Holt, the
Law Enforcement Academy significantly expanded its
advanced training program. More than 230 days of advanced programs were presented in 1990–91, marking a
50 percent increase in this area. Innovative programs
such as the Executive Development Series and the Criminal Investigator Series were unique offerings in the law
enforcement community. A jail management course was
the only course of its kind being offered in the state.
Lesson plans, handouts, and visual aids in current use in

1991

EVENING PROGRAMS INITIATIVE BEGINS WITH FALL 1991 SEMESTER.

the basic program were upgraded and improved. The classroom was equipped with a VCR and monitors.

The Division graduated 166 students from the basic program, representing 20 percent of all law enforcement academy graduates in the state. Also, during this time, the Law Enforcement Academy graduated its 100th session of the Basic Training Program. The Academy was selected to host the Federal Probation Officers Firearms Instructors School; it also hosted one of the two National Rifle Association schools, which was approved for college credit.

* The Adult Student Office, under the direction of Carroll Tingle, conducted research by developing and using a psychometric instrument titled College Success of Non-Traditional Students (CSNS) standardized and administered to an intact sample of adult students at the University. The purpose of the study was to determine if there was a significant correlation between preparation for re-entry to college and academic performance in college. The instrument is now used with new students to predict their readiness for school.

A milestone for Enriching the Adult Student Environment (EASE) was reached during this time as it was recognized as an official campus organization. Student Life provides the group with financial support, office space, and a mailbox. EASE meets weekly in the adult student resource room in Martha Parham West. The group interacts to provide support for members and to gain information through sessions covering such topics as study skills, stress management, creative thinking, financial aid, and time management.

The Adult Student Office had the unique opportunity

1991

REGGIE SMITH NAMED ASSOCIATE DEAN FOR THE COLLEGE OF CONTINUING STUDIES; CONTINUES AS DIRECTOR OF INSTRUCTIONAL PROGRAMS.

---

to counsel a handful of male students requiring special assistance in managing course work as they were called to participate in Operation Desert Storm in the Persian Gulf War. An adult student newsletter, "For Adults Only," was developed. Sent to selected adult students, the newsletter was edited and dispersed by students.

During the fall 1991 meeting, Dr. Snider more tightly focused the long-range goals he had previously set forth by announcing goals for the coming fiscal year. These included two or three "realistic goals to be attained by September 30, 1992" by each division. Significant among these goals were

* developing three new college and three new high school courses in Independent Study; increasing enrollment by 5 percent; establishing an advisory committee for high school and college programs
* relocating all offices of Administrative Services on the second floor of Martha Parham West; completing the biannual College-wide physical inventory; filling vacancies arising from retirement of two critical staff members, Bettie Copeland in budget and Joanne Miller in registration services
* streamlining the Law Enforcement Academy's offerings of advanced courses with the goal of offering courses that generate an 80 percent success rate based on the criteria of program quality, enrollments, and finance; enhancing the Academy's teaching facilities in Martha Parham West by refurbishing one additional classroom; establishing an advisory committee to increase the community awareness of LEA activity
* facilitating 700 or more conference-type activities in the Bryant Conference Center during 1991–92; strengthening the joint marketing and sales effort with the Sheraton Capstone Inn; operating the Center at a level that will preclude any further financial subsidy from the University after 1991–92

* increasing, through Instructional Programs, enrollment in the Evening Program by 50 percent and adding at least one new degree program; expanding the Gadsden Education and Research Center programming in both credit and noncredit areas; enhancing the Montgomery-area offerings with a wider variety of programs in fields such as courses in special education, social work, and library services
* completing, through Cooperative Education, an in-depth analysis of its continuing student growth pattern vis-a-vis the decline in funding that currently exists in order to determine the most appropriate direction for future programming and operational decisions; expanding the Government Intern Program in Montgomery by 20 percent and seeking continued funding for the Southeastern Training Center for Cooperative Education
* tripling student enrollments in QUEST through Educational Telecommunications; doubling the number of QUEST sites located throughout the state; developing sites in adjoining states; assisting the University and The University of Alabama System in administering the IITS during 1991–92
* redirecting 10 percent of Safe State activity from inspection services to onsite training and safety program management assistance; updating and expanding the environmental laboratory to enable performance of four additional laboratory procedures; increasing gross revenues of open-market training and conference activities by 20 percent
* implementing Uni-Link through the Division of Professional and Management Development Programs to offer at least five premier, noncredit professional development

1991

BCC HOSTS 600 CONFERENCES, CONTINUING TO GROW AFTER FOUR YEARS IN OPERATION.

CCS

THE COOPERATIVE EDUCATION DIVISION CONDUCTS CO-OP INTERVIEW DAY
TWICE A YEAR SO THAT EMPLOYERS AND PROSPECTIVE CO-OP STUDENTS CAN MEET
WITH ONE ANOTHER FACE-TO-FACE. APPROXIMATELY 50% OF THE STUDENTS
WHO GO THROUGH CO-OP INTERVIEW DAY ARE PLACED. UPON GRADUATION,
MORE THAN 90% OF CO-OP STUDENTS ARE OFFERED PERMANENT EMPLOYMENT BY
THEIR CO-OP EMPLOYERS.

programs during 1991–92; increasing income by at least
5 percent; increase contract programming with both
federal and state government; initiating new programs;
increasing emphasis on the production and sales of educational video tapes and materials

In closing, Dr. Snider noted that the College had served
60,000 people in seminars, workshops, credit courses, and
other offerings during 1990–91, an accomplishment in which
he felt all College staff could take pride.

By the deadline date of September 1992, virtually all the

1991

AS OF FALL 1991, THE INVENTORY OF PROGRAMS AT THE GADSDEN CENTER INCLUDES
MORE THAN 25 COMPLETE GRADUATE DEGREE OR CERTIFICATION PROGRAMS.

---

goals set forward by Dr. Snider in fall 1991 had been achieved or were well on their way to being achieved, despite funding restrictions that resulted from University wide proration and reduced enrollments resulting in part from a sluggish economy and the Gulf War crisis. Heading toward the 1992-93 academic year, with national predictions for education budgets somewhat grim and local proration a reality that forced cuts in all areas, the College of Continuing Studies remains strong, yet flexible enough to meet the challenge of providing high-quality, innovative continuing education programs for adult learners.

Bettie Copeland

"AMIDST ALL THE PAPERWORK AND THE MANY DETAILED TASKS, BEING ABLE TO WORK WITH SUCH WARM AND INTERESTING PEOPLE HAS MADE IT ALL WORTHWHILE."

PHOTOGRAPHY BY EARL

Bettie Copeland began working at what was then called Extended Services in 1971. Until 1984, she was an administra-

---

1992

COLLEGE OF CONTINUING STUDIES SIGNS THREE-YEAR LEASE FOR CLASSROOM AND OFFICE SPACE IN THE BIRMINGHAM JEFFERSON CIVIC CENTER TO SERVE AS A POINT OF CONTACT AND CLASSROOM FOR THAT AREA OF THE STATE. WEEKEND COLLEGE, PROFESSIONAL DEVELOPMENT, AND QUEST COURSES ARE SCHEDULED THERE.

---

tive assistant in the Dean's Office. Working in the administrations of Deans Drewery, Bryan, Prisk, and Snider she saw the progressive and successful growth of the College of Continuing Studies.

From 1984 until 1991, she served in the Office of Budget and Planning. When she retired in December 1991, she was Budget Coordinator and Assistant Director of Budget and Planning. Reporting to the Director of Budget and Planning, Copeland had major responsibilities for the College's $6,000,000 budget.

* * * * *

The Future of Continuing Studies

Dr. Snider and the staff of the College of Continuing Studies are well aware that demographics, technology, and a more information-oriented society will pose the greatest challenges for the College in future years. The aging population will mean more adults entering or returning to college; technological advances will necessitate more and more frequent professional updating or even career changes, which will in turn require further education. And the exponential growth of the information society will mean that people must continue to educate themselves simply to keep up with the accelerated pace of events on all fronts.

The College of Continuing Studies faces a tough challenge, but as it has evolved over the course of the twentieth century tough challenges have frequently spurred its growth. The

---

1992

MASTER OF SCIENCE IN AEROSPACE ENGINEERING VIA QUEST AVAILABLE IN THE FALL SEMESTER, PENDING APPROVAL.

---

financial limitations faced by all of the education community are no less real for continuing educators. But continuing educators are positioned to explore alternative forms of instruction through technological means and, thereby, become important leaders in the struggle to provide the invaluable commodity of education to adult learners. Infused with the entreprenurial spirit, continuing educators may be willing to take the risks to facilitate extension of the University's resources that will help ensure the institution's vitality in the next century.

1991
SINCE THE BLOODBORNE PATHOGENS STANDARDS WENT INTO EFFECT IN DECEMBER 1991, SAFE STATE HAS PROVIDED INFORMATION AND ASSISTANCE ABOUT COMPLIANCE WITH THE NEW RULE TO APPROXIMATELY 2,000 ALABAMA EMPLOYERS AND MANAGEMENT PERSONNEL IN THE HEALTH CARE INDUSTRY. THE AGENCY HAS BOTH SPONSORED AND PARTICIPATED IN DOZENS OF SEMINARS AND MADE OVER 220 ON-SITE VISITS IN CONNECTION WITH BLOODBORNE PATHOGENS INFORMATION.
1992
THE COLLEGE MEETS VIRTUALLY ALL OF ITS 1991-92 GOALS DESPITE SEVERE BUDGET RESTRAINTS AND REDUCED ENROLLMENTS.

Award for Teaching Excellence

The College of Continuing Studies presents the Award for Teaching Excellence annually to a person who has made outstanding contributions to continuing education programs through teaching and leadership. The award was established in 1985 by Dr. Dennis P. Prisk, dean, and is a continuing award. Recipients from 1985 to 1992 are

1985
Dr. James L. Taylor
College of Commerce and Business Administration

1986
Dr. Nathan L. Essex
College of Education

1987
Dr. Hazel F. Ezell
College of Commerce and Business Administration

1988
Jerry Patterson
University of Alabama at Birmingham

DR. PHILIP M. TURNER RECEIVED THE 1991 COLLEGE OF CONTINUING STUDIES'
AWARD FOR TEACHING EXCELLENCE FOR HIS WORK WITH CONTINUING
EDUCATION PROGRAMS IN LIBRARY SCIENCE AND INFORMATION STUDIES.
(L-R) DEAN JOHN C. SNIDER HOSTED THE AWARDS LUNCHEON FOR DR. TURNER
AND HIS WIFE, LIS, UNIVERSITY PRESIDENT E. ROGER SAYERS, AND OTHERS.

1989
Dr. Richard Crow
School of Social Work

1990
Dr. Carol Schlichter
College of Education

1991
Dr. Philip M. Turner
School of Library and Information Services

1992
Dr. Robert K. Leigh
College of Education

COLLEGE OF CONTINUING STUDIES
THE UNIVERSITY OF ALABAMA

Mission and Goals

With the creation of its Extension Division in 1919, The University of Alabama acknowledged, as part of its role as a comprehensive institution, a commitment to the continuing education of lifelong learners. This historical commitment provides the foundation for the activities of today's College of Continuing Studies whose programs allow individuals to continue their education, develop their skills, and enrich their lives. The College is a center of excellence that delivers the resources of the University to the people of the state, region, nation, and world. The College is the University's most direct and flexible instrument for meeting nontraditional educational needs.

The College of Continuing Studies creates and delivers opportunities for learning that people can use through their lives. To meet its commitment to lifelong learning, the College has established the following goals:

1. Provide accessible credit and noncredit programs.
2. Offer degree programs for the part-time student that may differ in structure from customary degree sequences, but not in quality.

3. Develop relationships that promote teaching, research, and service with government agencies, community organizations, professional associations, and the business community.

4. Establish professional and paraprofessional educational programs for profession and career development.

5. Develop certificate programs for clientele who seek advanced knowledge, but not necessarily a traditional degree.

6. Create a process to identify and meet the learning needs of diverse populations through innovative methods, curricula, and schedules.

7. Broaden the scope of programs offered in-state to include those of a regional, national, or international nature.

8. Advocate within the University community policies and programs that respond to the changing needs of its citizenry and develop a plan for continued assessment.

9. Serve the University as a resource center for applied research through its resident expertise and facilities.

10. Initiate and maintain cooperative relationships with other institutions of higher education and organizations dedicated to adult and continuing education.

11. Support The University of Alabama and its system in its educational efforts.

12. Provide leadership in the field of continuing education.

13. Incorporate modern telecommunications technology in the delivery of programs to people of the state and the nation.

14. Enhance the research, teaching, and public service missions at the University through a state-of-the-art residential conference center.

SOURCES

Archives and unpublished manuscripts

Research for this book included examination of existing archives of the Extension Division and the College of Continuing Studies from 1919–92. Some of these archives (from the beginnings of extension in 1919 through the midpoint of Dean Drewry's era in the early 1970s) are accessioned in The University of Alabama's William Stanley Hoole Special Collections Library. Included in these accessioned archives are enrollment reports, annual reports to the president of the University, copies of the *Extension News Bulletin* and *Extension News* from the 1940s, 1950s, and 1960s, a multitude of proposals and summary reports, and a wide variety of program brochures and direct mail pieces.

Other archives from the remainder of the Drewry era through the Prisk era, ending in 1989, and the 1989–90 Hudson interim are located on the sixth floor of Martha Parham West and in the dean's office. Documents from this time period also include enrollment reports, annual reports to the president, correspondence, proposals, news releases, and brochures.

From 1984 to 1990, a newsletter called *Spectrum* was published for the College of Continuing Studies, as were annual reports for distribution as promotional pieces. These publications would be useful to anyone wanting more in-depth information about the College during these years. Also, a summary report prepared for the dean's office in January 1989 was extremely helpful in preparing Chapter 7. These will be included in archives from this period.

The papers of Clarice Parker, made available to the College at the time of the establishment of the Clarice Parker Scholarship in 1988, were consulted for verification of facts from the early years, 1922–44.

The unpublished history of the Division of Extended Services (drafted circa 1974 by Jill Fussell for Dr. Drewry) is based extensively on the Parker history for the early years. This was used as the basis for Chapters 1–4.

Notes and manuscripts used in the preparation of this book will be included in archives in the Hoole Special Collections.

Photographs

Photographs were collected from the Hoole Special Collections, the College of Continuing Studies art department archives, University Television Services, and University Relations photography department.

Interviews

Interviews were conducted with numerous former employees of the College, including Bethel Fite, Mary Coe, Col. Joe Gelwix, Dr. Robert Leigh, Dr. L. Tennent Lee, Prof. Ray Hollub, Dr. James Condra, Bettie Copeland, Dr. Galen Drewry, Dr. William Bryan, Charles Adams, and Col. Robert Springfield. Keith Barze and Jim Oakley from the College of Communication were also consulted. All current division directors and the dean of Continuing Studies were interviewed or submitted written summaries of their divisions.

Other works

The University of Alabama, a Pictorial History by Suzanne Rau Wolfe (University of Alabama Press, 1983) was extremely helpful in placing the extension and continuing education movement within the greater context of the development of the University. J. B. Sellers's *History of the University of Alabama*, vol. 1., 1918–1902, was a source of information about the early summer school.

Anyone wishing to know more about the development of continuing education from a national perspective is encouraged to read Rhofeld's *Expanding Access to Knowledge, Higher Continuing Education* (National University Continuing Education Association, 1990).

INDEX

ABOUT THE AUTHOR

Jeanie Thompson is Marketing Director for Instructional Programs in the College of Continuing Studies at The University of Alabama. She received her M.F.A. in Creative Writing from The University of Alabama in 1977 and has been the recipient of individual writer's fellowships from the state arts councils of Louisiana and Alabama. She has published *How to Enter the River* and *Litany for A Vanishing Landscape,* both works of poetry, as well as features, book reviews, and interviews with writers, artists, and educators.